RAISING
DRUG-FREE
KIDS
IN A DRUG-FILLED
WORLD

RAISING DRUG-FREE KIDS
IN A DRUG-FILLED WORLD

William Mack Perkins
Nancy McMurtrie-Perkins

Harper/Hazelden

1982

FIRST HARPER & ROW EDITION PUBLISHED IN 1986.

Library of Congress Cataloging-in-Publication Data

Perkins, William Mack.
  Raising drug-free kids in a drug-filled world.

  Bibliography: p.
  1. Children—Drug use. 2. Drug abuse—Prevention. 3. Parenting.
I. McMurtrie-Perkins, Nancy. II. Title.
HV5824.C45P47   1987   649'.4   86–45826
ISBN: 0-06-254811-5

---

86 87 88 89 90 HC 10 9 8 7 6 5 4 3 2 1

To our children—
Steve, Tim, Danny,
Kelly, and Shannon—
they were our teachers.

And to
all of the parents and children
we met on our
Walk Around America.

Contents

Acknowledgments

We wish to thank Ray Nordine, Executive Director of Family Plus, Inc., St. Louis Park, Minnesota. He was there, even before the Walk Around America began. He was the first to clearly point out to us the role parents can play in the prevention of, and intervention in, adolescent alcohol and other drug abuse.

Also, we wish to thank Roger Svendsen and Tom Griffin, Hazelden Cork Education and Health Promotion Services, Minneapolis, Minnesota. Their contributions regarding prevention and chemical health are deeply appreciated.

We also want to express our deepest appreciation to the contributors who kept the Walk Around America going for two and one-half years. Their kindness, thoughtfulness, and generosity made this book possible.

And finally we want to thank all of our family, and in particular our parents, Frank Dody, Billy and Christine Perkins, and the loving spirit of Mabel Johnson Dody.

Can you imagine what *they* must have gone through when their middle-aged kids announced they were quitting their jobs, giving away everything they owned, and going on a Walk Around America to talk about alcohol, other drugs, and kids?

Parents. God bless 'em all.

PART ONE

Note: Neither the publisher nor the authors represent themselves as authorities on legal issues. This book is for general informational purposes only. The users of this book should consult their own attorney concerning the legal rights and obligations of parents and children. When this book refers to drugs, alcohol is included as a dangerous, mood-altering drug.

A Parenting Story

(NANCY)

Let me tell you what happened in our family when Shannon, our fourteen-year-old son, became involved with alcohol and other drugs. It's a story of what not to do.

My husband, Bill, and I are both recovering alcoholics. We are also certified alcohol and other drug counselors with many years of experience working with family drug abuse problems. You would think that, with our personal experiences and professional training, we would have been able to spot adolescent drug abuse in our own family. But that's not what happened. What happened in our family happens in most families when kids get involved with alcohol and other drugs.

We began to experience a series of problems which increased in frequency and severity and left us feeling angry, scared, and confused. At times we felt like we were losing our minds. Our training and experience didn't help us at all. As a matter of fact, they got in our way and kept us from getting the help we needed. We thought we could handle the problem ourselves. This thinking kept us isolated and unwilling to reach out for help. And the problems grew worse.

During the next year and a half, while we were trying to understand what was happening in our family, Shannon was giving us all the signals we needed to identify the problem. They were the signals of adolescent drug abuse.

He was breaking curfew and sneaking out of the house in the middle of the night. He was skipping school and missing classes. When he would go to school, he would go late. His grades started to drop. His attitude changed. He became irritable, sarcastic, and argumentative. He changed his hairstyle and the way he dressed. He ate huge amounts of food. His eyes were often bloodshot. His personal hygiene deteriorated. He began spending most of his time in his room with the door closed. He changed friends. When his new friends came to our home he would take them upstairs to his room and close the door. When he talked on the phone he would face the wall and whisper. He stopped making eye contact. He avoided the rest of the family.

He also started lying to us. We had asked him several times if he was using drugs. He told us he wasn't. We wanted to believe him. We kept telling ourselves, "Shannon is a good boy; he doesn't lie." And that was true. Shannon was a good boy, and he didn't lie until he started using drugs!

Along with the lying, Shannon broke every rule we set. We confronted his behavior time and again and threatened him with consequences. But we never followed through because each time we told Shannon he was going to suffer a consequence, he would react with an imploring, or angry, "THAT'S NOT FAIR!"

More than anything else in the world, Bill and I wanted to be fair, loving parents. And so we would say to each other, "Maybe he *didn't* understand the rule. Maybe we *aren't* being fair. Let's give him another chance." Then we would tell Shannon, "Okay, there won't be a consequence this time, but if you break any rule again, next time, for sure, there *will* be a consequence."

Because we weren't willing to follow through, we had to work twice as hard. We had to constantly make new rules. We tried to word each of these new rules precisely to avoid possible misunderstandings in the future. We ended up with a corkboard filled with rules, but they were empty words. Shannon knew it and we knew it.

Because we weren't willing to look at drug use as the cause of Shannon's unacceptable behavior, we had to find other reasons. First, we blamed it on dyslexia, an inability to read. Then we said it was an emotional problem. Then we decided it was boredom at school.

While we were trying to label the cause of our continuing problems, our family was growing further apart. Now our other children were withdrawing. They were angry and resentful over the attention Shannon was getting.

Also, Bill and I were blaming each other for our own pain and conflict. I would say to Bill, "Do something! Fix that kid! Straighten up this mess." Bill's response to that would be, "Shannon is fine. He's better now than he's ever been. You're overreacting!" We both felt crazy. Finally, the fighting between us got to be too much, and Bill and I separated. We stayed apart for three months, then moved back together promising ourselves that things would be better. But we soon discovered things weren't better; in fact, they were worse.

In my despair, I decided to call a friend. It was the first time since our problems began that I reached out for help. My friend listened to me crying into the phone for an hour. Then she said, "Nancy, it sounds like Shannon has a problem with drugs and your whole family is being affected." She suggested we take Shannon in for a drug evaluation.

To our surprise, Shannon agreed to go. It was determined in the evaluation that Shannon needed inpatient drug treatment. Again, to our surprise, Shannon agreed to go. We were relieved. The problem had been identified, and help was on the way.

There was one catch, however. The treatment center had a three-week waiting list. Shannon could not be admitted directly into treatment. We felt our fears coming back. We dreaded the thought of three more weeks of continuing problems.

The evaluation counselor suggested strongly that Bill and I get involved in Al-Anon. He also suggested no alcohol or other drug use and a ten o'clock curfew for Shannon during the three-week waiting period. The next two weeks passed without incident. Then, one night, just a week before he was to enter treatment, Shannon went to a party. Shortly before his curfew, we got a telephone call from him.

"I'm not coming home right away. I'm having too much fun, and I want to stay at the party."

Bill responded by saying, "Shannon, you know what the rule is. We expect you home on time."

"But Dad, I'm having such a good time and all my friends are staying."

In a firm voice, Bill said, "Shannon, you have a choice. You can come home on time, or you can stay at the party. If you choose to stay at the party and miss your curfew, we will pack your clothes and put them out on the front porch. Then we will lock the door. You will not be allowed back into this house until the counselors at the treatment center tell us you are ready to live here again."

It broke our hearts and terrified us to say those words. We knew if Shannon decided to stay at the party we would have to follow through.

Shannon made his decision. He decided not to come home. A few minutes after ten o'clock, we went up to Shannon's room, packed his clothes into a cardboard box and put them out on the porch.

We cried all night long, full of doubt and dread. The next morning we called the police and reported what had happened. They were helpful, offering to keep an eye out for him. We also called the county social service agency and told them what we had done. We suggest parents get professional legal advice, since preventing a child from returning home might violate child abuse and neglect laws in some states. In Chapter Six, we list some things to know before acting. Also, parents should remember that the consequences should fit the crime, and throwing a child out of the house for a minor violation of the rules isn't appropriate.

During the next week we didn't see or hear from Shannon. However, we did receive a call from one of our friends who had seen Shannon in a seedy, drug-dealing area of St. Paul, an area people avoid because so many shootings and killings take place there.

Adding to our mounting anxiety was the pressure we felt from our co-workers and families. They were upset by our intervention with Shannon. They asked, "How could you do that to your own child? How will he live? Where will he go? Where will he sleep? What will he eat?"

Now guilt was added to our doubt and fear. We prayed that we were doing the right thing. We had done what we thought best to interrupt Shannon's drug-use pattern. We hoped he would look at himself and see what drugs were doing to his life. Also, we had taken this action to give him a clear message, "You cannot use drugs and live in our home."

Bill and I felt incredibly alone, isolated even from each other. After two years of fighting, our relationship was empty. We were emotionally drained. We couldn't go to one another for help or nurturing. During the painful days and nights that Shannon was gone, Bill and I relied heavily upon our new friends in Al-Anon. Their guidance, understanding, and support got us through those difficult times and helped change our lives.

One week after we put Shannon's clothes on the porch, we received a call from the treatment center where Shannon had been evaluated. The caller said, "We have a young man here who says he's your son. His name is Shannon. He wants to be admitted to treatment. Can we have your permission to admit him?"

We cried with relief. That night, in the spring of 1979, we slept soundly for the first time in years.

The Walk Around America

(BILL)

Shannon completed the drug treatment program which he began that day in the spring of 1979. Since then, two more of our sons, Danny and Stephan, have been through alcohol and other drug rehabilitation programs, and our daughter, Kelly, has been through a residential program that addresses family issues concerning alcohol and other drug abuse. Our son, Tim, hasn't been through a treatment program, but he has always been an active part of our family's recovery process.

All of us have worked hard to make changes in ourselves, and that work has paid off. Today our family is healthier than ever. I am deeply grateful—beyond my ability to express it—for everything that has happened in our family.

It was with this feeling of gratitude that, shortly before sunrise on a Sunday morning in the spring of 1981, I began walking alone in a wooded path near our home in St. Paul. Fog drifted among the trees and bushes around me. Nothing else moved. All was quiet and still.

In that quiet moment, I felt the presence of God around me. With reverence I spoke a prayer of gratitude: "I am so thankful for everything You have given our family. I wish there were some way I could pass on to others what we have been given."

Before my next step touched the ground, I saw in my mind what was to become the "Walk Around America" and a drug-prevention program that would reach parents nationwide. I returned home that morning and told Nancy about my experience in the park and about my wish to share what we had learned about alcohol, other drugs, and kids with other families around America.

She was reluctant to talk about such an idea. As I paced excitedly across the kitchen floor, already putting the pieces of the trip together, she said, "If this is something you have to do, I'll understand and I'll support you. But I like the work I'm doing here. Besides, for the first time in my life I have a dependable income and a comfortable home. I don't want to give this up." I asked her to pray about it. She said she would. Within the month, she decided to go.

During the next two years we worked together, planning and writing a drug prevention program we thought would be helpful to other parents. We included information from our personal experiences and our professional training. We worked late nights and long weekends to bring all of this information together. Finally, our program was ready, and it was time to begin the second phase of our work. It was time to give our program away.

This giving away of our work would take place during the Walk Around America, which would lead us across 31 states and take us more than 10,000 miles. We planned to stop in towns and cities along the way and present our program, free of charge, to all parents who would come and listen. It was going to be an exciting quest. We couldn't wait to get started.

On March 31, 1983, after saying good-bye to our family and friends, we filled our station wagon with camping gear and program materials and set out into the unknown. We had little money and no idea where we would eat or sleep. We were stepping out on faith, and faith proved to be enough.

During the next two and one-half years we presented our program to thousands of parents around the perimeter of the United States. We talked to groups ranging in size from five to more than 300. We talked in church basements, college classrooms, hospital auditoriums, community centers, and the Dirksen Senate Office Building in Washington, D.C.

In addition to sharing our own experiences, we wanted to ask other parents what they were doing to prevent and stop alcohol and other drug use among their kids. Most often, parents told us that basic, down-to-earth parenting tools worked best.

To the best of our ability, we have written those basic parenting tools into this step-by-step guide. Now we pass it along to you—from us, our children, and all of the parents and kids we met on our Walk Around America.

What Kind of Parent Has a Drug-Using Kid?

During our Walk Around America we met and talked with thousands of parents whose children were using and abusing alcohol and other drugs. All of those parents had one thing in common. All of them had thought, "It won't happen to us." None of them thought they were the kind of parent whose child would use drugs. Everywhere we went, those parents told us they once had a fixed image of what drug-using kids—and their parents— looked like. "We didn't fit that image," they said, "so we just couldn't see ourselves as the parents of a drug-using child."

When *you* think about drug-using kids, what image do *you* see?

What do those kids look like?

Do you see boys or girls?

How do they dress?

How do they behave?

Where do they live?

Now, what image do *you* see when you think about the *parents* of those drug-using kids?

Do you see parents who live in the suburbs?

Do you see happily married couples?

Do you see successful professional people?

Do you see well-known, active members of the community?

Most parents don't see those kinds of healthy, successful images when they picture parents of drug-using kids. The parents we met told us they saw images of broken homes or absent parents. They saw images of parents who were uncaring, unloving, and probably alcoholic themselves. These parents just couldn't see themselves, or their family, in that picture.

Cindy, a mother we met in Michigan, told us her family's story:

"I still can't believe it sometimes. It may sound silly, but we were a picture-perfect family. Jack and I were still in love after twenty years of marriage. His business was going great, and we had just moved into a lovely new home. Jennifer and Jack Jr. were doing well in school, and both of them were active in school sports.

"We even looked perfect. Our friends kidded us about it. They said we looked like a Norman Rockwell painting when we sat together in church. And the truth is, I was proud of that image. I *wanted* to look like a Norman Rockwell painting.

"Then, when Jennifer was fifteen, she started smoking marijuana with some of her friends from church. No more Norman Rockwell for us."

Her voice trailed off as she looked out the window of her new home, across the freshly mowed lawn. Then she said, "I've heard people say no child is immune to the drug epidemic. Well, no parent is immune either."

No parent is immune. We saw that everywhere we went in America. We saw parents from all walks of life whose children were involved with alcohol and other drugs. Mayors, ministers, secretaries, salespeople, school principals, truck drivers, pilots, and unemployed parents—all of them had trouble with kids who were using and abusing alcohol and other drugs.

These are parents who, like millions of others, are affected by a tragic national statistic: 90 percent of the young people in America use alcohol and drugs before they graduate from high school, and 60 percent of those young people use them regularly each week. These statistics tell us what kind of parent has a drug-using kid. EVERY kind of parent can have a drug-using kid.

What Can Parents Do?

One night at the Parents' Program, while we were talking about prevention, a woman raised her hand and said, "I'm a recovering alcoholic and I believe I was born alcoholic. I don't know if alcoholism and other drug addiction can be prevented."

We don't know either. There is a lot of controversy about the causes of drug addiction—and just as much controversy about prevention. We've talked with researchers, physicians, social workers, drug counselors, nutritionists, chiropractors, psychiatrists, and recovering drug addicts all around the country regarding this controversy. They all have different ideas about what causes addiction.

Some believe it's inherited.

Some believe it's a learned behavior.

Some think it's based in poor nutrition.

Some see it as a lack of willpower.

Some believe it's a physical disease.

Some say it's a mental disorder.

Some believe it's a combination of physical, mental, and spiritual causes.

We asked these people, "Do you believe drug addiction can be *prevented*?" Some said yes. Some said no.

We don't know if it can be prevented, but we *do* know parents can take steps to *try* to prevent and intervene in the problems caused by drug use. The following thirteen chapters are suggested as a guide toward reaching that goal.

PART TWO

1. Avoid Reacting to Drugs in Ways That Don't Work

The first step in preventing problems caused by drug use is to recognize and avoid what doesn't work. Here is the "top ten" list of what doesn't work, according to parents who learned the hard way.

Enabling

Many parents said their biggest mistake was to step in and rescue their children from the consequences of their drug use. When a parent rescues, it's called enabling.

Parents enable by not confronting drug use, by allowing a child to use at home, by making excuses for inappropriate behavior, by bailing kids out of jail (when they're guilty), by getting their child out of trouble at school, by calling in sick for them at work or school, by giving them money and not keeping track of how they spend it, and by not questioning them when items are missing from the home.

One night, after we had talked about enabling in our Parents' Program, a father, who looked to be 70 years old, said, "I've been enabling my son's alcohol use since he was fifteen years old." As he talked, tears formed in his eyes. "He's 40 years old now, and I'm still doing it. I'm paying his rent and insurance, bailing him out of jail, and paying off bad checks.

"My son always promised if I helped him, he would stop drinking. I've helped him as much as I can. I've spent my entire life's savings trying to help him. But he's still drinking."

When we rescue our children from the consequences of their drug use, we enable them to continue in that use. Parents can work with legal authorities to stop enabling their children. For instance, if parents become involved with the legal system, a court may realize a child's problem is drug use, and the child might receive the needed help. Our court system can be used to force a child into a treatment program where they can get help, even if they don't want it.

Denial

We met a mother in Michigan who told us there are no drugs in the junior high or senior high schools her children attend. She has a thirteen-year-old and a sixteen-year-old. Because of her denial, she is not prepared for the possible drug use by her children.

Denial of a drug problem *won't* make it go away. Denial *will* prevent parents from taking action.

Reacting

Some years ago we had a client who reacted to her son's *first* drug use by following him around, writing down everything he did. When the mother came to see us, she was carrying a stack of notes documenting her son's every move for the past month.

"You have to put my son in drug treatment!" she said.

We told her we couldn't put her son in treatment without first doing an evaluation. She agreed to bring her son in.

During the evaluation her son admitted to smoking pot, but only the one time his mother knew about. Believing we may have missed something, we asked another counselor to make a second evaluation. The second evaluation also failed to turn up any history of drug use other than that one time.

We called the mother in and reviewed the evaluation outcome with her. We told her we couldn't recommend treatment for her son based on that one incident of drug use. As we talked, we could see the panic rising in her eyes. We soon discovered *why* she was reacting so strongly. She was a single parent, with total responsibility for raising her son. She said she was terrified of drug use because she had heard so many horror stories about drugs and kids.

She needed basic, sound information about alcohol and other drugs. She also needed support for herself, so we referred her into counseling and to a parents' group. Her son, after weeks of being followed, was relieved and grateful.

Threats

Some parents use threats in an attempt to keep their children from using drugs. They say, "If I ever find out you're using drugs, I'll beat you within an inch of your life." Or they say, "If I ever catch you using drugs, you'll never leave this house again!"

Threatening doesn't keep kids away from drugs; threatening keeps kids away from parents. Parents should also be concerned about their moral and legal obligations. Parents who are unreasonable in their discipline, abuse a child, or ignore the need for medical or drug treatment are violating their children's rights.

Scare Tactics

Some parents try to scare their kids away from drugs. They say, "If you use drugs you could overdose and die." Or, "You'll get kicked out of school . . . become a prostitute . . . end up in jail. . . ."

Most of the kids we met around America said they don't pay any attention to these warnings. They believe their parents are overreacting. They say, "That won't happen to me."

Providing Alcohol and Other Drugs for Kids

Some parents believe kids are going to drink no matter what, and it would be better if they drink at home. Some of these parents allow teenage beer parties in their homes. Some even provide the beer.

One angry parent in San Antonio told us, "One of the reasons these parents allow beer parties at their homes is to keep their own children safe. They don't want *their* kids driving drunk or riding in a car with a drunk driver. But the kids who go to those parties have to drive there and back. *Those* kids are in danger."

In Maryland a parent told us, "My fifteen-year-old son went to a party at his friend's house, and there was a keg of beer in the backyard. Kids as young as twelve were drinking and getting drunk. My son said the boy's parents bought the beer for the party. When I asked where the boy's parents were during the party, he said, 'I don't know. I didn't see them.' "

It's legal in some states for minors to drink at home or as part of a religious ceremony, but parents may still be liable if they then allow children to drive or do anything that could cause damage.

Parents have told us they are confronting adults who serve alcohol to minors—and they are taking action to stop it. They are reporting these violations to authorities and are following up with the authorities to make sure action is being taken.

If you are an adult who is concerned about other adults serving alcohol to minors—confront it. If you are an adult who is providing alcohol to minors—stop it.

Bribery

Some parents try to bribe their kids into not using drugs. They say, "I'll buy you a new stereo, but you've got to promise me you'll never use alcohol or other drugs." Or they say, "I'll buy you a car, but you've got to promise you'll never drink and drive."

Bribery doesn't stop drug use. Bribery opens the door for parents to be manipulated.

Minimizing

A mother in Alabama told us her son had nearly died after an alcohol overdose. The mother minimized this crisis by saying, "He was out with friends just having a good time. All kids drink once in a while, don't they?"

Using Guilt

Some parents try to use guilt to keep their children from using drugs. They tell their children, "If you really love me, you won't use drugs." Or they say, "I would have a nervous breakdown if I ever found out you used drugs."

Using guilt doesn't prevent drug use, it just makes kids feel guilty.

Fighting between Parents

When kids use drugs, parents fight. They fight about whether a problem exists or not. They fight about what to do or not to do. They fight about whose fault it is, and they fight about who's responsible for the problem.

When parents fight they take the focus off the drug use. Drug-using kids know this, and use it. Kids have told us they manipulate fights between their parents to draw attention away from themselves and their drug use. A young girl in Florida told us, "When I could get a fight started between my parents, they would get off my back. Usually one of my parents would take my side. When that happened, I could do anything I wanted to!"

If these reactions to alcohol, other drugs, and kids don't work, what *does* work? Chapter Two begins to answer that question.

2. Be Aware That Early Drug Use Is a Matter of Decision

"By the time I left the hospital with my new son," the father said, "I had been told how to protect him from mumps, measles, and whooping cough, diseases which *might* threaten him during the years he was growing up.

"But no one told me about the drug epidemic! No one told me how to protect my son from the one disease which was *certain* to threaten him."

The father paused for a moment and then continued. "When my son got involved with drugs, I discovered the drug epidemic is a different kind of problem. It is *destructive decision making*. My son was *deciding* to use drugs. He was *deciding* to be a part of the epidemic. Until I understood that, I couldn't help him."

That father, who had intervened early in his son's drug use, had come to understand an important distinction between abuse and addiction: with early drug use, kids have *choices*.

Listen to what the Reverend Phil Hansen, director of one of the nation's oldest and largest drug rehabilitaiton centers, says about the difference between early adolescent drug use and addiction.

"When parents discover that their children are using or abusing chemicals, I believe there is a tendency to seek out treatment for chemical dependency. I personally believe that an overwhelming majority of adolescents using drugs are not chemically dependent, but are misusing and abusing drugs. Misuse and abuse are *voluntarily decided-upon activities*."

The following graph, called the Spectrum of Drug Decisions, illustrates this by showing the four progressive stages of alcohol and other drug use. During the first three stages, from "no use" to "use" to "abuse," a person makes choices about whether to use or not use, whether to abuse or not abuse. It is only after a person crosses the line into addiction that choices are gone.

SPECTRUM OF DRUG DECISIONS

NO USE	USE	ABUSE	ADDICTION
CHOICES			NO CHOICE

We know two facts about crossing that line into addiction. Both of these facts can help parents understand early drug use.

First, we know addiction is progressive; it takes continued use, over a period of time, to reach addiction.

Second, we know only 10 percent of the population becomes addicted—90 percent never cross that line into addiction.

If we put these two facts together, we can conclude that the majority of early users are not addicted—they are using and abusing alcohol and other drugs as a *choice*. It is *vitally important* to understand the difference between addiction and decision making; it is the key to knowing what to do and how to do it.

The most effective response to addiction is to get the addicted person to qualified, specialized addiction treatment. The most effective action we can take to deal with decision making is to influence those decisions with all the power we have as parents.

Understanding your power as a parent, and knowing how to use that power to influence drug decisions, begins with knowing what you're up against—the powerful and compelling reasons why kids decide to use drugs.

Chapter Three looks at these reasons.

3. Understand Why Kids Use Drugs

Why do young people get involved with alcohol and other drugs when they know it can ruin and destroy their lives?

Kids *do* know how destructive alcohol and other drugs can be, because they live with it every day. Most high school students can tell you about sitting in a classroom where other students were so stoned they didn't know what was going on around them. Most high school seniors have lost a friend or classmate to an alcohol- or other drug-related accident or suicide. Kids see the consequences of drug use firsthand. And yet they continue to get themselves involved. And we parents are stuck with the question, "Why?"

We wanted to get some direct answers to that question, so we went into drug treatment centers around the country and asked the kids. Here are some of their answers.

"I didn't think it would happen to me."

Kids everywhere told us they didn't believe *they* would be victims of drug abuse. They don't pay any attention to research and statistics. But this attitude isn't exclusive to kids. Many adults don't believe drug warnings, either. Read the warning printed on a package of cigarettes. Then look around at all the adults who smoke.

We adults read drug warnings, but we dismiss them. We say, "It won't happen to me." We shouldn't be surprised when our kids do that too.

"All of my friends drink."

How many parents have heard that? When kids say, "All of

my friends drink," they are telling us intense peer pressure is bearing down on them. Unfortunately, some parents don't recognize just *how* intense peer pressure is, and as a result, they minimize it.

We heard one mother say, "If he just had a good, strong self-image, he could say 'no' to his friends who drink."

Another mother said, about her daughter, "Well, she should just find other friends. She doesn't need those kinds of friends."

There are some parents who *do* know how intense adolescent peer pressure is because they recognize the peer pressure in their own lives. Listen to this father from New York: "I feel peer pressure when I say 'no' to sugar. Like a lot of people today, I try to keep my sugar intake to a minimum. I do fine until I visit a friend and they bring out the sweets, like a cherry pie made from 'Grandmother's secret recipe.'

"When they first offer me the sweets I say, 'No thank you.' But they insist. They push the sweets closer to me and say, 'Oh, come on. Try just one piece.'

"I tell them, 'I'm sure it's delicious, but I'm trying to watch my weight.'

"They say, 'You? Don't be silly! You look great. One little piece won't hurt you. Besides, I spent all day baking this.'

"Finally, I take a piece and say, 'well, alright . . . just this one piece.' "

That's adult peer pressure. Now substitute alcohol and other drugs for the cherry pie, and that's adolescent peer pressure.

"The people I admire most drink and use drugs."

A sixteen-year-old boy in Mississippi told us, "My mother knew sports were the most important thing in my life. She tried to use my love of sports to keep me away from drugs. She told me drugs would keep me from performing at my best when I played football.

"But I had been reading the sports page since I was a little kid. I knew some of the best athletes in America were using drugs. Guys who could run a hundred yards in less than ten seconds were using drugs. They were doing great. Drugs weren't hurting *their* performance. So I didn't pay any attention to my mother's warnings, and I started using drugs when I was fifteen."

Parents are role models too, and we must remember we can greatly influence our children's values and behavior through how we live our lives. We should live by the values we teach; we should try to *instill in* our children these values rather than *impose on them* our beliefs. If we abuse alcohol or other drugs, we are only showing them by our own example that it is acceptable behavior.

"It's forbidden."

Some kids told us they first used alcohol or other drugs just because it was forbidden. But we don't need kids to tell us that forbidding something makes it all the more compelling. If you forbid something, people will give away their souls just to try it. The attraction toward things which are forbidden is deep-rooted in most of us, including our kids.

Jokingly, we tell parents, "The urge to try the forbidden is so much a part of a kid's nature that we could use it to accomplish just about anything. If we were given the canned spinach account just for the United States, the first thing we would do is try to get the FDA to put spinach off limits to kids nineteen and under.

"Can you see what would happen? You'd be going into the grocery store and some sixteen-year-old would be hanging around the doorway. As you walked into the store, the kid would whisper, 'Hey mister, would you pick me up a six-pack of spinach while you're in there?' "

This may be a farfetched example, but it makes the point: forbidding something creates curiosity, attraction, and defiance.

Television, Movies, and Music

Television

Television is a "drug pusher." Think about it: what's a pusher supposed to do? Glamorize the product and get someone to try it, right? That's exactly what television commercials about alcohol do. Take a close look at a television beer commercial. They begin with the warm, rosy glow of a fading afternoon. Then the hard-working people in the commercial gather in their favorite bar and begin to relax as the workday ends. These are nice people. These are pretty people; all of them are happy and laughing. *Everybody* in these beer commercials is happy because everybody likes everybody else. And you can just tell that all these people would like you, too, if you were with them, drinking in that bar.

Now, as you think about that commercial, picture this scene in your mind. A father is watching a football game on TV. A five-year-old child is sitting in Dad's lap, just enjoying being there. Duirng a game time-out, a beer commercial comes on the screen.

What do you think that child sees? Just what Dad sees: laughter and good times. Deep inside, desire is created. There is only one difference between the child and the father. The child is not old enough to buy beer yet, but he or she will be old enough one day.

Movies

One night in Louisiana, we asked the audience if they knew who Cheech and Chong were. With only that quick mention of their names, a young boy sitting in the front row burst into laughter and almost fell out of his chair. Cheech and Chong are funny guys who make funny movies. But the problem is, their movies make smoking marijuana look funny, too. This is another compelling influence to use drugs.

Music

Read the song titles, and listen to the lyrics. Much of the music sings about drugs, and kids love the music. It's a powerful connection, a powerful influence.

"To be somebody"

When we presented our program in Rancho Mirage, California, there were teenagers in the audience from a nearby halfway house. We asked them to tell the adults the reasons why they began using drugs. One sixteen-year-old boy, in a nervous but determined voice said, "I wanted to be somebody. All my life I felt inferior. I always felt left out, like I didn't have any friends. Drugs made me feel like I belonged. I had friends when I used drugs."

(BILL)

As I listened to that boy, I remembered the first time I drank alcohol. In a deeply personal way, I understood exactly what he was talking about. I got involved with alcohol and other drugs for the same reason: I wanted to be somebody.

I was born in a small town in Kentucky. The part of town I grew up in was, literally, on the wrong side of the tracks. Kids who lived there were called "crawbats," and in my hometown that was the worst thing a kid could be. When kids from the craw went over to the other side of town, the adults there would chase us away and tell us to go back "where we belonged." In the craw, kids got tough quick or they were in big trouble. I didn't get tough at all.

I had a sweet face, big brown eyes, skinny little arms and legs. Each morning I had to try to make it across the craw to school. In the afternoons, the *sissies* in my neighborhood would chase me home! It was not fun being me. I spent a lot of days and nights—and years—alone.

Then, one Friday night when I was fifteen years old, some older boys asked me if I would like to go with them to a local roadhouse and drink beer. I would have gone anywhere, with anyone, to do anything, to have friends, to be accepted.

That night, we drove out to that roadhouse, and those older boys bought me my first beer. As I drank that beer, my nervousness slowly went away, and the anxiety in my stomach disappeared. I began to laugh and talk. I danced with a girl for the first time in my life. Then I got into a fight with a bigger and older boy, and I discovered some athletic ability I hadn't been aware of!

You can imagine what happened in such a small community. By Monday morning everybody in my high school was telling the story about how I got drunk and won that fight. For the first time in my life, *I was somebody!*

It was a negative way to become somebody. But for all those years, I felt left out and ill at ease around people. Suddenly I discovered simply by drinking and getting drunk, I could have friends, be accepted, and be somebody. That's a compelling reason for a fifteen-year-old to drink.

"It feels good."

Kids everywhere told us this is the number one reason they use drugs. And yet, some parents don't want to talk about this most powerful of all drug influences. We've had parents tell us, "Don't say that. That will just put ideas into kids' heads. There's nothing good or attractive about drugs!"

And we say, "Know your enemy!" Alcohol and other drugs *can* make kids feel good, and kids know that. When we ignore or deny that, we run the risk of destroying our credibility with our kids and putting distance between ourselves and them.

The fact that drugs can make users feel good is illustrated in this graph, called The Feeling Chart.

PAIN | NORMAL | EUPHORIA

The Feeling Chart is taken from the book *I'll Quit Tomorrow*, by Dr. Vernon Johnson. Dr. Johnson says most of us live our lives in the middle range, feeling "normal." Then, with the first use of alcohol or other drugs, the central nervous system becomes sedated and a sense of euphoria is created.

That's what happens to most young first-time users. They go out with friends, use drugs for the first time, the sedative effect takes place, and they experience a mood swing from normal to euphoria. They begin to feel good.

Then, intoxicated or stoned, they go home. Because their parents are not looking for anything unusual, they get into the house without getting caught. Quietly, they go to bed.

The next morning they wake up, and the first thing they remember is how good it felt to be high the night before. Now it's just not going to happen that a kid will say, "That was great! . . . I'm never going to do that again." They remember what being high felt like, and they say, "Where can I get more of *that*?"

These are powerful, compelling drug influences—don't underestimate them. They weigh heavily each time our children make a decision about drug use. Today it's imperative that we prepare for these influences by developing parenting skills and tools which will make us an even greater influence.

Chapter Four will tell us how early we can begin developing these tools.

4. Practice Early Drug Problem Prevention

How early can drug problem prevention begin? We asked that question at each of the Parents' Programs we presented. Some of the answers were: "during grade school . . . before kids start school . . . at birth . . . during pregnancy . . . before pregnancy."

These answers lead to an important point: the *earlier* we begin alcohol and drug problem prevention, the better.

Drug Prevention Begins before Pregnancy

Because little is known about the relationship between alcohol and drug use by parents at the time of conception and their child's predisposition to chemical dependency, it is best for the prospective parents to not use alcohol or other drugs during the time they are trying to conceive.

Dr. Carlton Fredericks says, "Many drugs cross the placental barrier and many of them are capable of causing harm." Birth defects and deformities are traceable to alcohol and other drug use by the parents before and during pregnancy.

Alcohol and other drugs are antinutrients and rob the fetus of vitamins and minerals needed to develop properly. Also, when drugs cross the placental barrier the fetus can become physically addicted prior to birth. Parents who avoid drugs will prevent a child from being born physically addicted.

We usually think about the mother's health before and during pregnancy, but the father also has a responsibility to remain drug free and well-nourished. Alcohol or other drug use by the father at the time of conception can affect the chromosomes carried by the sperm and affect the baby.

Drug Prevention Continues following Birth

(NANCY)

Shortly after my children were born, I began medicating them with one drug after another. I was, in the truest sense of the term, a drug pusher. I gave my children phenobarbital for colic, medications for teething, liquid aspirin for fever, decongestants and cough syrups for colds. My children grew up knowing that when they had a headache, stomachache, cough, or fever, I would try to fix the problem with a drug.

Also, during this time my children saw me taking prescription and over-the-counter drugs on a regular basis. I gave my children a very clear message: if you are uncomfortable, physically or emotionally, take a drug. You'll feel better. I believed I was doing the right thing; I thought I was helping. Now I know that many of the drugs I gave my children contained caffeine or alcohol— they were mood-altering chemicals!

There are drugs available that contain neither alcohol nor caffeine. Since new medications are introduced every year, and children can react individually to drugs, parents should ask their doctor for advice before giving any medication to their children.

Nurture before Medicating

We should not be so quick to medicate our children. When they complain about physical or emotional pain, take time with them before going to the medicine chest—nurture before medicating. If they have headaches or fever, we suggest you have them lie down where it's quiet, and put a cool cloth on their heads. Give them some water or juice to drink. While you're sitting with them, ask some questions about what's going on in their lives.

When my children came to me with physical complaints, it was often because of a crisis in their lives. They were having problems with their friends, with schoolwork, with teachers, or with me. I discovered children's emotional pain can become physical pain because of the difficulty they have in expressing their thoughts and feelings.

If your child's complaint continues after nurturing, contact a physician. *Never* medicate on your own because it could mask symptoms of a serious health problem.

We suggest the following guidelines regarding medications:

• Ask your physician how to treat your child without using drugs; ask what you can do concerning diet, vaporizers, rubs, etc.
• Be sure to tell your physician about *any* medications your child is currently taking. Drugs which are safe to take alone can be dangerous when taken in combination.
• Don't give children medicine prescribed for someone else.
• Find a pharmacist you trust to discuss medications.
• Ask questions about the medicine prescribed. Ask how medication is to be taken (at what time, with or without food), how long the medication should be taken, and possible side effects.
• Follow the prescribed dosage exactly.
• If your physician prescribes a medication for your child which you believe could be mood altering or cause dependency, ask for the medication to be changed. If your physician refuses, get a second opinion.

Parents of young people in recovery from drug dependency need to be especially vigilant about the medications their children take. Prescribed mood-altering medications can lead to relapse.

Prevention Includes Avoiding Other Mood-Altering Chemicals

Caffeine and nicotine are not commonly thought of as mood-altering drugs, but they are. They act as stimulants to the central nervous system and change the body's chemistry. Adults or children using nicotine or caffeine can experience anxiety, nervousness, restlessness, hyperactive behavior, and other mood changes.

We visited with a family in Georgia whose one-year-old child carried a baby bottle filled with cola containing caffeine with him all evening. The child was running around the room, pulling at his mother's clothing, screaming for attention, tossing toys and newspapers into the air, and banging on the furniture with his bottle.

The mother turned to us and said, "I don't know what to do with him any more, his behavior keeps getting worse, and lately he's not sleeping."

We asked her, "Do you think it might be the caffeine in the cola he's drinking that's causing him to be so overactive?"

She answered quickly, almost in a panic, "No, it can't be *that*!"

Her reaction was understandable. If she acknowledged the caffeine in her son's cola was causing his overactive behavior, she would have to take away the cola, and that would cause a whole new set of problems.

Caffeine and nicotine are addictive. Recent studies reveal that people who stop using caffeine and nicotine experience psychological and physical withdrawal symptoms, including headaches, dizziness, fatigue, nausea, irritability, and craving. Kids told us they drink six or more cans of cola containing caffeine a day. Each twelve-ounce can of cola contains 32–38 milligrams of caffeine. For many of these kids, using this amount of caffeine was the beginning of getting "hooked" on mood-altering chemicals.

Food Additives Can Be Mood Altering

When we presented our Parents Program to the NASA staff at Langley Field, Virginia, some of the staff members talked about their children's behavioral and emotional problems. They said they had found a direct relationship between their children's behavior and the additives in their food and drinks. They specifically mentioned the red food coloring in a popular artificial, tropical fruit drink. When they removed the artificial fruit drink from their children's diet, their behavior improved noticeably.

Sugar Can Be a Mood-Altering Substance

We heard controversy all around the country about the effects of additives, preservatives, and other substances added to our food. There is one substance, however, which many agree is causing a vast array of problems, particularly among our children. That substance is sugar.

Here are excerpts from an article printed in *The Dallas Times Herald*. It reflects the beliefs and opinions of many of the parents and professionals with whom we talked.

School Does Major Study on the Effects of Sugar

The fifth grader was overweight, had behavioral problems in the classroom and his schoolwork was suffering.

In a conference with his parents, the principal began asking about the child's diet. When told he ate a lot of sugary snacks, the principal gently pointed out that what a child eats can affect his or her behavior.

Sugar, in particular, may contribute to hyperactive behavior and severe mood swings.

Alexander Schauss, Director of the American Institute for Biosocial Research, believes that *many teens and preteens turn to drugs and alcohol to make themselves feel better because their poor diets make them feel rotten.*

"When the amount of sugar in sodas is added to the sugary cereals, the candy, the sugar added to ketchup, canned and processed foods, it is not unusual for children to be eating the equivalent of between 50 to 90 teaspoons of sugar a day."

This causes the blood-sugar level to go up and down, as the body tries to burn up the excess sugar. These "ups and downs" can cause behavior mood swings from hyper-happy to tired and depressed.

"It is a known scientific fact that refined carbohydrates, such as refined sugar, deplete the level of vitamin B-1, a vitamin essential to maintaining the integrity of the central nervous system," said Schauss.

"Is it any wonder that diets heavily laden with refined carbohydrates foster aggression, hostility, irritability, inability to control emotions, and violence?"

Food Allergies Can Also Cause Mood Swings

Do your children insist on having certain foods or drinks? If so, it's possible they may have an addictive allergy according to Dr. Lendon Smith in his book *Feed Your Kids Right*. In some children, common table foods such as milk, eggs, wheat, corn, nuts, and sugar can create allergic reactions that can cause mood changes and addictive behavior. Other substances that can cause addictive allergies are caffeine, tobacco, drugs, and environmental chemicals, just to name a few.

An addictive allergic reaction to food can cause a child to crave the food to which he or she is allergic. This craving is similar to the craving for drugs experienced by a drug addict. After the child eats or drinks the food that causes the reaction, the craving is satisfied and the child feels better. A few hours later, the withdrawal process begins and the child experiences withdrawal symptoms including fatigue, irritability, moodiness, fearfulness, confusion, anger, and inability to concentrate. In an attempt to relieve these symptoms, the child seeks out the food which he or she is allergic to, and the cycle continues.

Dr. Smith says, "Part of the explanation for an allergic addiction is that an allergy to something in the food makes the blood sugar go up for a while and afterward to plummet downward. This subsequent uncomfortable feeling encourages the victim to ingest the offending food again.

"They are rewarded by a return of energy and a sense of relief; they have learned what to eat when they feel depressed or out of sorts."

Food Addiction and Drug Addiction Can Be Similar

I clearly saw the devastating emotional effects of mood-altering substances during the years I worked with people in recovery from alcohol and other drug abuse. Many of these recovering people came to see me after they had been drug free for periods of a few months to a year or longer. They came to me because they were still experiencing many of the same mood swings and behavior problems they had when they were using drugs.

My interviews revealed that they had given up alcohol and illegal drugs, but continued—and often increased—their use of nicotine, caffeine, and sugar. I would stress to them the importance of not using these substances, and those clients who did this and ate more nutritiously reported a positive change in how they thought, felt, and acted.

Avoiding all mood-altering substances is the beginning of alcohol and other drug abuse prevention in the family. Chapter Five will examine ways to continue practicing prevention at home.

5. Practice Ongoing Prevention through Nutrition

While we were making the Walk Around America, we saw a striking and widespread change take place in the understanding of the role nutrition plays in the prevention and treatment of drug abuse. Nutrition had been misunderstood, ignored, or simply rejected as not being relevant to drug problems. Now—in a relatively short period of time—it has become an accepted component of both prevention and recovery. The human service professionals using nutrition for prevention and treatment include physicians, psychologists, penologists, youth counselors, and school officials.

Dr. L. Ann Mueller and Katherine Ketcham in their book *Eating Right to Live Sober* say,

> The power of nutritious food and vitamin and mineral supplements to promote healing and health in recovering alcoholics is supported both by research and clinical experience.
>
> The research solidly links diet to mental as well as physical health, and the evergrowing evidence points clearly to the connection that what we eat directly influences how we think and feel.

Using nutrition as an alcohol and drug abuse prevention tool is supported by substantial research and documentation. As long ago as 1949, Dr. Roger J. Williams, a biochemist now at the University of Texas, demonstrated that laboratory animals would choose alcohol if certain vitamins were eliminated from their diets. When the vitamins were restored to their diet, the animals stopped drinking alcohol.

Dr. Williams says, "From all the facts relating alcoholism to biochemical factors and nutritional deficiencies, *it becomes clear that whatever measures we take to prevent alcoholism, the neglect of the nutritional approach cannot be justified.*"

The Declining Nutrients in Our Foods

Using a sound nutritional program is more important today than it's ever been before. Today the soils in which our foods are grown is vastly different from the soils which grew foods 100 years ago. Continuous planting, failure to rotate crops, failure to allow fields to lie fallow for a season, and natural weathering have depleted the once-rich earth of many trace elements. Food plants will continue to grow in these nutrient-depleted soils, but the health and well-being of the people eating them will be affected.

In his book *Mental and Elemental Nutrients*, Dr. Carl C. Pfeiffer says, "Foods continue to lose nutrients during the time required for harvesting and shipping crops. Even under the best storage conditions, vegetables kept too long decrease significantly in nutritive value."

The Price We Pay for Convenience Foods

Processing, too, decreases the vital nutrients in our food. Dr. Pfeiffer, referring to food processing, says, "Canned and frozen meats and vegetables, prepared bread and cereals, refined flour and sugar, which remain attractive and succulent on supermarket shelves for considerable periods, represent a modern convenience. But the price paid for this convenience amounts to a drastic reduction in available nutrients."

With the addition of nutrient-depleting preparation, the food reaching our tables is often devoid of nutritional value.

The Invisibility of Poor Nutrition

The suggestion that we need to make changes in our diet to obtain sufficient nutrition can be surprising because most of us *look* so well fed. But, as Dr. Donald R. Land, a nutritional consultant specializing in addiction, states, "Nutritional deficiencies are manifested by emotional and psychological symptoms *long before physical signs appear.*"

In *Mental and Elemental Nutrients*, Dr. Pfeiffer says, "The well-nourished American is a myth . . . malnutrition may afflict up to 80 percent of the nation's population."

Nutrition As a Parenting Tool

Using nutrition as a drug prevention technique is an idea whose time has come. Parents can practice good nutrition with the whole family and help their children reduce the risk of having drug problems. Here are some suggestions for a family nutrition program that will work toward alcohol and other drug prevention:

Read Labels

Today, reading labels on food is a *must* in practicing good nutrition. Too often, little attention is given to the quality of the food we eat or the way our food is prepared. Sometimes we don't even know if what we are eating is actually food or just a food look-alike.

One day, while we were grocery shopping, we picked up a package of cheese puffs for dogs and read the ingredients listed on the outside of the package. Then, we went over to the snack food section and checked the ingredients on a package of cheese puffs for humans. To our surprise, we discovered there was more nutritional value in the dog food than in the food for humans.

That discovery started us thinking. We began looking around the store, checking the foods we serve our children. It didn't take long to realize that a lot of the foods manufactured and marketed for our consumption are quite literally not fit for a dog!

Most dog owners feed their dogs food which will produce a shiny coat, good teeth, and strong bones. They feed their dogs food based on the nutrients needed to assure good health. Don't we have a responsibility to practice equally sound nutrition with our own *children*?

Select the Least Processed Foods Available

Dr. Lendon Smith says, "If a food has been packaged, processed, added to, stabilized, emulsified, colored, or preserved, you know it's out of nature's hand."

In Texas, a prevention specialist told us the following story about an experience he had with food additives and preservatives.

"A friend of mine stopped by my desk at work one day and gave me a packaged cake. Instead of eating it right away, I put it in my desk drawer thinking I'd eat it later. I forgot all about it, and slowly it made its way to the back of my desk drawer, where it remained. A year later, when I was cleaning out my drawer, I found the cake. When I took it out of its wrapper and felt it, it was as soft and seemingly fresh as the day I got it!"

It makes us wonder what effect additives and preservatives have on our bodies if they keep a cake soft for a year.

Use Whole Grain Products Rather Than White Flour Products

White flour products and white rice are stripped of most of their nutrients during processing. Few of these nutrients are replaced, leaving white flour products deficient in nutrition.

One hundred percent whole grain breads, whole wheat spaghetti and macaroni, brown rice, and barley are excellent sources of protein, plus many more nutrients. Whole grain cereals including oats, rice, and wheat are good breakfast cereals which have not been laden with sugar. Whole wheat products are found in health food stores and can be bought inexpensively in bulk form in food co-ops.

Serve Fresh Fruit Juices in Place of Soft Drinks

There are two nutritional advantages in making this switch. First, you eliminate a lot of sugar, caffeine, food coloring, and food additives. Second, you substitute healthy foods for these potentially harmful substances.

Use Natural Sweeteners in Place of Refined Sugar

Honey contains some vitamins and is absorbed less rapidly into the system. It's relatively free of pesticides and artificial flavors, colors, and preservatives. However, honey is still very sweet, so use it sparingly. Because honey contains bacteria spores which may adversely affect infants, it's best to check with your pediatrician before giving honey to a child under one year old.

Use Legumes as a Source of Protein

Lentils, peas, beans, and other legumes are an excellent source of protein, minerals, and vitamins, and they are relatively free of chemicals. They make inexpensive, easy-to-prepare, delicious meals.

Serve Chemical-Free Meats and Poultry

It may seem impossible to purchase meat and poultry which is not full of antibiotics and hormones which have been fed to animals to stimulate growth, but it can be done. Some butchers sell meat and poultry which are chemical free. If you can't find these at your butcher, check with your local food co-op; they usually post where meat and poultry without additives can be purchased.

Serve Raw Nuts and Seeds

Kids love raw sunflower seeds, pumpkin seeds, peanuts, almonds, and cashews. These foods are all good sources of protein. Nuts and seeds make a great snack or they can be added to baked goods, salads, vegetables, and hot dishes.

Serve Healthy Snacks

Encourage your family to eat lots of fresh fruits and raw vegetables; they are good sources of vitamins and fiber. Whenever possible, buy organically grown fruits and vegetables from your local food co-op. In organic farming no pesticides are used. Serving snacks of whole grain bread or crackers, peanut butter, cheese, and popcorn instead of cookies, potato chips, or candy will improve your family's diet.

Making this change in a diet will eliminate the negatives and accentuate the positives. Eliminating "junk food" will encourage a more healthful diet and make for healthier kids.

Adolescents Need Sound Nutrition

All of us need the same nutrients in our diets, but some of us need more nutrients than others. We each have our own unique biochemistry, and because our life-styles vary, our foods vary.

Also, our stresses are different. According to Dr. Lyndon Smith, one of the highest sources of stress is adolescent peer pressure. Personal adjustment problems and socioeconomic problems also create adolescent stress. Stress factors cause blood sugar to fall, place a heavy demand upon the adrenal glands to produce cortisol and adrenalin, and require a constant replenishment of the expended nutrients.

In his book *Can Alcoholism Be Prevented?*, Dr. Roger J. Williams says that by eating the right foods in the right proportion and taking daily vitamins and mineral supplements the susceptibility to alcohol abuse can be reduced.

When we began to make changes to improve our family's nutrition, we began with snacks, junk foods, and soft drinks. We told our kids, "We've decided not to buy any more sugary snacks, junk food, or soft drinks with caffeine and sugar. If you want those foods and drinks, you'll have to buy them with your own money."

Our kids didn't like these changes at first, but we held firm, while educating them about why we were making the changes. We believe one of the many positive benefits of practicing good nutrition and having well-nourished children is the reduced risk of alcohol and other drug problems. That one benefit makes practicing good nutrition worthwhile.

6. Learn All You Can about Alcohol and Other Drugs

Most parents told us they began learning about alcohol and other drugs by reading books, pamphlets, magazine articles, and anything else they could get their hands on. You can get the information you need to acquire a sound education about alcohol, other drugs, and kids by contacting the following resources:

Hazelden Educational Materials
Box 176
Pleasant Valley Road
Center City, MN 55012
1-800-328-9000

Will send a catalog of publications on alcohol and other drugs, prevention, and parenting

Families In Action
3845 N. Druid Hills Road
Suite 300
Decatur, GA 30033
(404) 325-5799

Publishes a quarterly newsletter, "Drug Abuse Update"

Committees of Correspondence
57 Conant St., Room 113
Danvers, MA 01923
(617) 774-2641

Publishes newsletter exchanging information on drug abuse issues; also recommends other reading

PRIDE (Parents Resource Institute for Drug Education)
100 Edgewood Avenue
Suite 1002
Atlanta, GA 30303
1-800-241-9746

Publishes a quarterly newsletter and catalog of resource materials

In addition, parents can contact state agencies for help.

Know the Signs of Drug Use

These signs can be helpful in identifying an alcohol or other drug abuser. However, these signs can also apply to a child who is *not* using drugs. Be cautious before making accusations.

- Red eyes—the use of eye drops such as Visine or Murine
- A distorted sense of time
- A drop in school performance; not necessarily from As to Ds, but from As to Bs and Cs
- Caring less about everything: school, sports, music, or hobbies
- Eating extremes—loss of appetite, eating huge amounts of food, or craving sweets
- Withdrawal from family, mood changes, irritability, hostility
- Impaired memory or judgment
- Chronic cough, chest pains
- Depression, feelings of loneliness, paranoia
- Fatigue and loss of vitality
- "Flattened" speech and expression
- Sleep disturbances
- Menstrual irregularities
- Secretiveness, vagueness about social activities
- Less attention paid to cleanliness of body, hair, and clothes
- Disappearance of money or items of value from the home
- Difficulty in fighting off common infections
- Drug-oriented graffiti on school notebooks and/or drug messages in school yearbooks or memory books
- Drug paraphernalia: a pot pipe, rolling papers
- Use of incense to hide the sweet burnt odor of pot, breath fresheners, room deodorizers

Be watchful. Early awareness is the key to early intervention.

Attend Drug Education Programs

Drug education programs are usually sponsored by Chemical People Task Force Groups, alcohol and other drug education/rehabilitation programs, mental health centers, churches, and civic groups. Many of these programs are free and are advertised through public service announcements or in the local newspaper.

At each of our Walk Around America programs, at least one parent would come up and tell us, "I was so busy I almost didn't come. I'm so glad I did."

We encourage parents to make time in their busy schedules to attend these community drug and alcohol education programs—and bring a friend!

Gather Information from Community Resources

We suggest you call the following agencies and ask all the questions that could help you prepare for an alcohol or other drug-related emergency or problem. Gathering all the information you can before a crisis will allow you to *act* rather than *react*.

Here are a few suggested resources and questions you should ask:

Detoxification Center or Hospital
What is the minimum age you accept a child into detox?
How long do you keep a child in detox?
What does it cost to put a child through detox?
Can I visit your facility?
Do you provide alcohol and other drug assessment and referral?
If not, where can I get a drug assessment for my child?

Social Services/Juvenile Court
What exactly is my responsibility as a parent when my child continues to use drugs and endangers his or her own and other people's lives?
What will happen if I lock my child out of the house because of his or her drug use? Will you place my child in protective custody?
In what situation can I be arrested? Prosecuted?
Can I have my child committed to alcohol and other drug treatment against his or her will?

Police
If my child is arrested for alcohol or other drug use, what will happen?
If my child is put in jail, what happens if I refuse to come and get him or her?

Alcohol/Drug Rehabilitation Centers
What is the minimum age for children coming into your treatment center?
Do you provide detoxification?
How long does treatment last?
How much does treatment cost?
Do you have a program for family members?

This early planning may seem unnecessary right now, but as any parent who has dealt with a drug emergency can tell you, the time you invest *now* will prepare you to respond effectively in the future.

Join a Parents' Group

Many parents told us they initially resisted joining a parents' group. They were too busy, too tired, or didn't want to get involved. But the main reason they didn't join—at first—is they didn't think *they* needed a parents' group. That's what we thought, too. But, like those other parents, when we did join a parents' group we found support and direction that changed our lives.

After we became involved in a number of parents' groups we found that, generally speaking, there are two different kinds of parents' groups. *Self-help groups* hold regularly scheduled meetings where group members are encouraged to talk about their problems and express their feelings. These groups usually have a suggested guideline, or program, which members use to work on their problems. The group offers support and encouragement as members "work the program" and make changes in their individual and family lives.

The second kind of group is often referred to as a *prevention, education, and legislation group*. These groups focus on local, state, and national issues regarding alcohol and other drug abuse. They support and sponsor a wide range of projects including school-based alcohol and other drug prevention programs, community drug education, and political action aimed at alcohol and drug legislation.

We suggest you find out what kinds of parents' programs are available in your community—and which ones you want to join—by talking with members of the groups in your area. Some of the parents' groups listed below can be found in the yellow pages or white pages of your telephone book. If you can't find them there, contact the national office to find out the location of the group nearest you—or how you can start a group in *your* community.

Here are the national offices of four *self-help* organizations:

TOUGHLOVE
P.O. Box 1069
Doylestown, PA 18901
(215) 348-7090

Al-Anon Family Groups
P.O. Box 862
Midtown Station
New York, NY 10018-0862
(212) 302-7240

Families Anonymous
P.O. Box 344
Torrance, CA 90401
(213) 775-3211

Nar-Anon Family Group Headquarters, Inc.
P.O. Box 2562
Palos Verdes Peninsula, CA 90274
(213) 547-5800

Here are the national offices of three *prevention, education, and legislation* organizations:

National Federation of Parents for Drug Free Youth
8730 Georgia Avenue, Suite 200
Silver Spring, MD 20910

PRIDE (Parents Resource Institute for Drug Education)
100 Edgewood Avenue, Suite 1002
Atlanta, GA 30303
1-800-241-9746

Families in Action
3845 N. Druid Hills Road, Suite 300
Decatur, GA 30033
(404) 325-5799

Get involved!

7. Prepare Your Child to Enter a Drug-Filled World

(BILL)

Have you ever had one of those incredible parenting experiences when, just for a moment, you clearly saw how much joy, wonder, and love your child had brought into your life? I had one of those moments years ago when I was a student at the University of North Carolina and my son Danny was just four years old. One winter morning, I awoke early to finish a term paper before the noise of the day began.

Suddenly Danny came bursting out of his bedroom, yelling, "Snow! Snow!" I looked out the kitchen window and saw the ground was covered with a fresh, deep blanket of snow. Danny's hands trembled as he pulled at his boots and struggled to get his coat over his pajamas. His face was flushed, his eyes intense. Outside on the porch, his dog, Charlie, sensed the excitement and was jumping up and down, grabbing looks through the kitchen door window. Finally dressed, Danny bounded out the door, tripped over Charlie, and leapt from the porch with the dog right at his heels. The two of them ran, Danny laughing and Charlie barking all across the new-fallen snow.

Pushing my term paper aside, I sat at the kitchen table, alone in that early morning hour, and watched my son play. For him, it was a time of pure and perfect joy. For me, it was a perfect parenting moment. Then, behind me, the radio clicked on, activated by the timer set for seven o'clock. The news carried the story of a manned space capsule scheduled for reentry that morning.

This was the mid-1960s and the manned space flight program had reached the point that fear and concern had been eliminated from orbiting, but reentry still brought a period of high concern.

During the period of reentry the astronauts had to leave the loop-ing safety of orbit and go through a period during which com-munication failed and risks increased.

As I watched Danny and listened to the radio, I felt a vague, cold fear rising. Then Danny laughed again and ran out of sight. I knew what had caused my fear; I had seen, somewhere in my mind, the comparison between Danny and the astronauts who were about to begin their earth entry.

Today he was out there, circling in that small and safe back-yard that was his orbit. He was in direct communication with his family. He was orbiting, looping. Safe and sound. But he, like the astronauts, would soon begin earth entry. School, sports, new friends, and new things to do that would take him out of his safe, familiar orbit. He, too, would go through a time during which communications failed and danger increased. And one of the big-gest dangers my son would face would be drugs. I knew that much, but that was about all I knew. I had no idea how to help him prepare for that.

The awareness which had interrupted and ended my perfect parenting moment had given me insight only into the risks my child would face, not what I could do about those risks. It was only years later, after Danny had entered his world and become involved with drugs, that I learned about the things parents can do to provide their children with the knowledge, skill, and strength they will need to make their entry into—and their way through—a drug-filled world. Here are four ways *you* can help your child through the time of earth entry.

Talk with Your Child about Drug Influences

Don't let your kids get "blind sided" by drug influences. Tell them what's ahead. Use the list of drug influences outlined in Chapter Three to tell your child what other kids will be saying about drugs and drug use. We need to tell our children—before other kids tell them—that alcohol and drugs can temporarily make them feel good. We need to let our children know—ahead of time—that some of their friends will use drugs and pressure them to use too. If our kids know what's coming it will help them to plan and prepare.

Listen to Your Child

It's important to talk to our children about alcohol and drugs. But we need to listen, too. Ask some questions to get them talking:

"How do you feel about drugs?"
"What concerns you the most?"
"What are you learning about drugs?"
"Are there drugs in your school?"
Then listen. Don't debate or argue. Just listen.

Help Your Child Develop a Plan to Say "No" to Drugs

We can help our children prepare to say "no" to drugs by role playing with them. We can take the role of a friend or someone else who is offering them alcohol or other drugs and let our child practice saying "no" with us.

We can also help our children prepare to get out of drug-using situations by helping them plan excuses to leave those situations. Have them use any excuse. Tell your children you'll back them up. Have them say they have to go to the dentist, or you expect them home to clean out the garage. Tell them to say whatever necessary, and then to call you. Tell them you'll come to get them, anywhere, anytime.

Be Loving and Supportive

Saying "no" to drugs sometimes causes kids to feel loss and pain. Old friends go away, and new friends are hard to find. Sometimes saying "no" can be lonely.

During these painful times, love and support from home become crucial. Don't minimize or deny your child's pain; offer your child support by saying, "I know this is a difficult time for you. I can see you're hurt. I want you to know I support the decisions you're making not to use drugs, and I love you."

Love is an important part of helping our children to say "no."

Unfortunately, when kids become involved with drugs, love does not conquer all. There are thousands of loving parents all around America who can tell you that from personal experience. Parents also need to take firm action. That takes us to Chapter Eight.

8. Set a "No Use" Rule

Because we were in recovery from alcoholism and were working as chemical dependency counselors, we assumed our children would know we didn't want them to use drugs. Because we only assumed, like many other parents, we didn't set a rule.

"How do I set a rule about alcohol and other drug use?" parents ask. "What guidelines should I follow?"

The guideline many families follow is to set a rule which conforms to local, state, and federal laws.

- No use of alcohol by a minor
- No possession or use of any illegal drugs
- No use or purchase of cigarettes by a minor
- "No illegal use" is a good guideline upon which to base the no use rule. It's a good place to begin.

However, the legal issue alone won't prevent many kids from using alcohol or other drugs. As a matter of fact, putting *anything* off limits to kids, and using a forbidding tone can cause a young person to challenge the no use rule. Simply saying "Because it's illegal . . . Because I said so! . . . Because that's the rule! . . . " isn't enough. We need to provide our children with sound, logical, and reasonable information they can use to form their own no use decisions.

In addition to the legal considerations, there are other valid and important reasons why young people should abstain from mood-altering drugs. These reasons include all of the negative consequences that can result from alcohol and other drug use. Some of these negative consequences are outlined in the following list. When setting the no use rule, set aside enough time to discuss in a caring, respectful manner how these consequences could affect both your child and your entire family.

Physical

- Alcohol and other drugs are the cause of thousands of teenage automobile accidents, suicides, and drownings.
- Alcohol abuse can cause permanent, irreversible brain damage.
- Alcohol abuse causes dizziness, staggering, slurred speech, double vision, and vomiting.
- Alcohol abuse adversely affects the brain, central nervous system, liver, pancreas, digestive system, and adrenals.
- Alcohol and other drugs are antinutrients and rob the body of vitamins and minerals.
- Drug users can develop a tolerance which requires them to use more to achieve the same effects.
- Marijuana contains chemical ingredients which are fat soluble and can stay in the body tissue up to a month following one incidence of use.
- Marijuana smoke contains cancer-causing chemicals.
- Marijuana irritates lungs and impairs their ability to expel bacteria and other foreign substances.
- Cocaine use can cause vomiting, rapid increase (then decrease) in blood pressure, changes in body temperature, dryness of mouth, dizziness, tremors, and vertigo.
- Nicotine use depresses appetite and deadens taste buds.
- Nicotine stimulates adrenal functioning, causing blood sugar levels to go rapidly up and down.
- Nicotine use can cause headache, dizziness, and irritability.

Psychological

- Alcohol and other drug use causes temporary impairment of brain functioning resulting in inability to "tune in" to real feelings and emotions.
- Mood-altering chemicals impair emotional growth.
- Alcohol and other drug use causes loss of inhibitions.
- Chemical abuse retards emotional growth and coping skills.
- Alcohol and other drug abuse interferes with personality development.

- Alcohol and other drug use can result in psychological dependence.
- Drug abuse can create abrupt mood changes.

Mental

- Alcohol and other drug use reduces judgment.
- Mood-altering chemicals lower ability to concentrate.
- Abuse of alcohol and other drugs cause temporary and permanent brain dysfunction.
- Alcohol and other drug abuse results in disorientation.
- Alcohol and other drug abuse causes memory impairment and loss.

School

- Alcohol and other drug abuse lowers reading comprehension.
- Drug abuse can cause short-term memory loss.
- Alcohol and other drug abuse reduces verbal and mathematical problem-solving skills.
- Abuse of mood-altering chemicals reduces academic interest and motivation.
- Alcohol and other drug abuse interferes with extracurricular activities.
- Drug and alcohol abuse increases friction with peers and teachers.

Family and Personal Relationships

Alcohol and other drug abuse can cause

- loss of intimacy and trust
- feelings of isolation and loneliness
- withdrawal from family and friends
- relationships formed with those who use drugs in a similar way
- relationships with family and friends to change from positive to negative

Spiritual

Alcohol and other drug abuse can cause

- losing belief in a "Higher Power" or spiritual self
- dropping out of religious activities
- lying to protect use of alcohol and other drugs
- stealing to finance drug use
- promiscuity related to alcohol and other drug use
- conflicts between values and behavior
- anger and blaming a "Higher Power" for personal problems

Sports

Alcohol and other drug abuse can cause

- loss of timing
- physical deterioration
- lack of motivation
- loss of stamina
- team unity split between "users" and "nonusers"

Driving

Alcohol and other drug use can

- slow down reaction time
- affect coordination
- impair vision
- reduce motor skills
- increase risk taking

Sexuality

Alcohol and other drug abuse can

- reduce male sperm production and mobility
- cause irregular menstrual cycles and egg production

In establishing the no use rule, share with your children what you've learned about alcohol and other drugs. In order to encourage cooperation, present your information in a loving and respectful way. But be firm! Let your children know that if they break the no use rule, there will be a consequence. It is not necessary to *what* the consequences will be or *when* a consequence will occur. It is necessary only to state, firmly and clearly, that there will be a consequence if the no use rule is broken. When you have finished setting the no use rule, have each child repeat back to you what you said. This will help avoid future misunderstandings.

When we talked about the no use rule during our programs, parents frequently asked these three questions:

"What about teaching kids responsible drinking?"

The question of teaching responsible drinking to kids always brings up two more questions for us.

The first question is, "How do you teach responsible drinking when drinking by a minor is illegal? How can *illegal* use be *responsible* use?"

The second question is, "Do you truly believe kids who use 'responsibly'—which usually means they limit their intake in front of their parents—will drink responsibly with their friends?" It is our personal belief, but a belief based on talking to a lot of kids, that this is a pretty naive expectation. It's not only kids who think that teaching responsible drinking doesn't work. Here's what a mother representing the National Federation of Parents for Drug Free Youth says about responsible drinking:

> NFP believes there is no such thing as 'responsible use' of alcohol when it is used by our youth. One reason is because alcohol is toxic to growing cells. Another problem is the addiction to alcohol. The younger a person starts to drink, the more chance of becoming chemically dependent.

The attempt to teach responsible use carries a clear message: "It is okay to drink!" Is that the message you want to give your kids?

"What about signing contracts to pick up kids when they're too drunk to drive?"

These contracts have two *big* problems. First, they give kids conflicting messages. These contracts say, in effect, "Don't drink

. . . but when you get drunk call home." Second, these contracts assume drunk kids *will* call home. It is a dangerous disregard of the pharmacological effects of alcohol to believe kids, *whose reasoning has been impaired by alcohol,* will do the reasonable thing when they have been drinking.

"How can I tell my kids not to drink when I drink?"

One way is to say to your kids, "In this house we use alcohol and drugs *legally, responsibly,* and *appropriately.*"

Legally means that there is *no use of alcohol by a minor* and no use of illegal drugs by anyone.

Responsibly means that if the adults in the family choose to drink, they do it in a responsible manner. It means an adult doesn't drink beer all day and then jump into the car and drive. That's not responsible.

Appropriately means that if adults choose to drink, they drink at an appropriate time and place, and in a responsible manner. Getting drunk is *never* legal, responsible, or appropriate.

In order to make sure the no use rule is being followed, we need to be watchful. We need to set a curfew and be awake when our kids come home. We need to watch for the signs and signals of alcohol and other drug use in our kids' actions and attitudes.

"Does this include searching my child's room or going through personal belongings?" some parents ask.

This is one of the most controversial questions that came up as we talked with parents. Some parents said, "If I had good reason to suspect that my child was using drugs—but I couldn't confront it because I couldn't prove it—I believe it would be my responsibility to look for drugs or paraphernalia, even if that meant searching the child's room."

Other parents voiced the opposite opinion. "I wouldn't destroy the trust between my children and myself by searching their room or clothing—or any of their belongings. I believe my children have a right to privacy."

In our family, *before* three of our kids became involved with drugs, we agreed with the parents who said kids have a right to privacy. We trusted our kids and played by the rules. That changed after our kids got involved with drugs.

Bill Cosby told a cute story about "playing by the rules." It's a story about the Revolutionary War, but it can be used to make an important point about parents, kids, and drugs. Cosby said that England lost the Revolutionary War to America because the two sides fought by different rules. "The British troops had to march in a straight line across an open field with a big red X across their chests . . . and they couldn't even shoot until they saw the whites of the American's eyes! The American soldiers, they got to hide behind the rocks and the trees and stuff. And they could start shooting anytime they wanted to!"

Cosby finished by asking, "Guess who won!"

Two different sets of rules. That's what happens in families when kids use drugs. In our family, we were playing by the old rules, but our kids weren't. Their rules protected their drug use. They were hiding behind excuses, evasions, and lies. They were shooting at us with guilt and manipulation. And they were winning!

Then, finally, after our son Shannon went to a drug rehabilitation center, we looked around his room. We found drugs and paraphernalia everywhere! In his closet, under his bed, between the mattress and spring, inside his stereo speakers, and pinned behind his curtains. Clearly, we hadn't been watching what was going on in our own home.

The no use rule requires parents to be alert and vigilant. It also requires that parents be prepared to confront any violation of the no use rule. Confrontation takes us to Chapter Nine.

9. Confront All Alcohol and Other Drug Use

We have a responsibility to our children, ourselves, and our families to confront all alcohol and other drug use by our minor children. When we fail to confront drug use, we enable the use—and the risks and problems associated with the use continue. The following guidelines are suggested for confronting alcohol and other drug use:

Don't Talk to a Child about Drug Use While the Child Is Drunk or High

Confronting kids who are under the influence of alcohol or other drugs can have negative results. Kids can either hear everything their parents say as lecturing and just tune it out, or they can become defensive, angry, and abusive. This can create a dangerous situation. Before talking to a child, allow enough time for the effects of the drugs to wear off. It's counterproductive to *talk* to a drunk or stoned child, but *action* is required.

Take an Intoxicated Child to a Detoxification Center or Hospital Emergency Room

In the case of a heavily intoxicated child, the recommended action is to take the child to a detoxification center or hospital emergency room. We suggest this action because intoxication is a medical emergency requiring detoxification.

If you doubt the importance of taking intoxicated kids to detox, here is the story of one father who failed to take such action. It happened in our hometown, St. Paul, Minnesota.

A young man who had been at a party got so drunk his friends decided to take him home. Afraid to face the young man's parents, the friends decided to put him in the family car parked in the driveway. Later that evening the father came home and saw the boy sleeping in the car. He opened the car door to awaken his son and smelled the odor of alcohol. He closed the car door and went into the house, deciding to let his son "sleep it off." The next morning when the boy didn't come into the house, the father went out to get him. He found his son dead.

Today our kids are mixing many kinds of drugs with alcohol. Drugs in combination with alcohol can produce a sedative effect which can continue and deepen during sleep. This can be fatal. We can no longer take the risk of allowing our children to "sleep it off." A detoxification center can provide drug screens on an intoxicated person, medically monitor that person, and take appropriate medical action.

Parents have often asked us, "Are you saying the first time my child comes home drunk I should take him or her to detox?"

Our reply is, "Yes. The first time."

They say, "Isn't that overreacting?"

Our response is it's not overreacting if it's part of your plan to deal with alcohol and other drugs. "If it's in your plan, it's *action*—not reaction." In addition to protecting your child's life, a trip to detox can have a second benefit. It will show your child you mean business. Most detox centers are not pretty and they don't smell good. Hopefully, this kind of experience will be a deterrent to future drug use.

Detox centers are listed in the telephone book under Detoxification Center or Receiving Center. If your book doesn't list either of these, call the police or your state's drug agency for information. Keep trying until you find the number, and do it now, before a crisis occurs.

No one wants to go to detox, and it can be a real struggle to get an intoxicated kid to go. Some parents will need help. Call friends or family members in advance, and ask if they would be willing to help you, anytime, day or night, take your child to get the medical help needed.

Monitor a Child Who Has Been Using Alcohol or Other Drugs

Most detox centers or hospital emergency rooms won't admit a child who is not heavily intoxicated. This leaves parents with the question of what to do with a child who has obviously been using drugs (he or she may be giddy, slightly unsteady, red eyed) but is not heavily intoxicated.

In these cases, the responsibility of monitoring children falls on the parents. To monitor children in your home, periodically check to make sure their breathing is steady and strong. Make certain they are sleeping on their stomach, with their mouth to the side; intoxicated kids can vomit in their sleep, and if they are lying on their back with their mouth turned upward, they can drown in their own vomit. If they begin to breathe in any manner which seems unusual, wake them up to make certain they can regain consciousness. If they can't be awakened, call the paramedics or an ambulance immediately.

Have Crisis Numbers Ready

You may never have to use crisis numbers. But have them ready and available—*written out and placed next to your telephone.*
Have these numbers ready:

- paramedics
- ambulance
- hospital emergency room
- family physician
- mental health center
- suicide crisis center
- detoxification center
- family and friends who will help

If an emergency occurs, the last thing you want to do is be looking through the telephone book for emergency numbers, especially at three o'clock in the morning.

Take Time for Yourself: Plan Your Confrontation

You've become aware that the no use rule has been broken. Now it's time to talk to your child. An important part of confrontation is taking time to plan, in advance, what you want to say and what action to take. This may be difficult, especially after seeing your child intoxicated or high. But planning, calmly and rationally, is necessary to bring about a constructive confrontation. Take time to calm yourself. Take time to talk to your spouse or a friend. Taking time will help you be more objective.

In planning your confrontation, ask yourself the following questions:

Where do I want a confrontation to take place?

Do I want someone else present? Who?

What evidence and information do I want to present?

What tone of voice do I want to use?

What do I want to say?

What do I want to happen (drug evaluation, drug treatment, family counseling) as a result of this confrontation? What consequences are appropriate?

The time you take here will pay off later.

Be Specific

When confronting your child about drug use, it is important to present information which is specific and relevant. The following questions can be used as a checklist for developing that information.

_____ Have you caught your child using alcohol or other drugs?

_____ Have you detected physical signs—alcohol on the breath, slurred speech, eyeball or pupil change?

_____ Have you found obvious signs such as liquor bottles or marijuana, pills, or other drugs in the bedroom, garage, or other places?

_____ Have your child's dress habits and personal hygiene significantly changed?

_____ Have your child's eating or sleeping habits changed?

_____ Have you missed money or objects that could be converted to cash? Has your child lied to you?

_____ Does your child spend a lot of time alone behind closed doors in the bedroom, recreation room, or other places?

_____ Has your child's personality changed noticeably? Are there sudden inappropriate mood changes (irritability, unprovoked hostility, giddiness)?

_____ Is he or she less responsible for chores, getting to school on time, household rules?

_____ Does your child seem to be losing old friends and hanging out with a drinking or partying crowd?

_____ Is there trouble at school—grades dropping, classes being missed, interest in school activities waning?

_____ Is your liquor supply dwindling? Does it taste like colored water? What about pills missing?

_____ Is your child in trouble with the law?

_____ Does your child react belligerently to comments, criticism, or remarks about his or her drinking or other drug use?

_____ Does your child get into fights with other youngsters?

_____ Are there signs of major medical or emotional problems (ulcers, gastritis, liver problems, depression, overwhelming anxiety, suicide talk)?

_____ Is he or she irresponsible behind the wheel of an auto?

_____ Does your child turn off to talks, television shows, or literature about alcohol, alcoholism, or drug abuse?

After you have developed the information you want to use in the confrontation, present the information in a respectful, but firm manner. Do not make accusations that you can't back up with facts or observation.

Stick to the Issue of Their Drug Use

When confronted with drug use, it's predictable that young people will try to manipulate the conversation away from their drug use by arguing, debating, or changing the subject. They do this by saying:

"You drink! How can you tell me not to drink?"

"You're overreacting, I only had _one_ beer."

"Research shows pot smoking isn't harmful."

When this happens don't get sucked in. Tell the child, "We'll talk about that later. Right now, we're talking about *your* alcohol and other drug use and how it is affecting your life and this family." *Don't debate!* When parents get into debates with drug-using kids, parents lose.

Be Prepared for Excuses, Promises, and Threats

Here's what one kid said about excuses: "Last summer my parents found some pot I left in the ashtray of my car. When they asked me about it, I said, 'That belongs to a friend of mine. He didn't want his parents to find it, so he left it in my car.' If you can believe it, my parents *fell* for that!"

Here's what another kid said about promises: "When my parents started talking about my drug use, I would promise them anything to get them to stop talking. I promised them I would see a school counselor . . . anything to get them off my back."

Kids use threats in an attempt to stop parents from taking action. Kids tell parents, "If you ground me, I'm going to run away." Or they say, "If you think I'm bad now, you just wait! This is nothing. I'll show you!"

The threat which calls for immediate action by parents is the threat of suicide. Each year more and more kids are committing suicide, and the age at which they are doing it is getting younger and younger. If your child threatens suicide, we recommend you take the child immediately to a crisis center, suicide center, mental health center, or an agency in your area that works with potential suicides. Get help immediately. A suicide or crisis center will assess the situation and make recommendations and a referral, if needed.

If your child is using the threat of suicide as manipulation, the long, drawn-out assessment and referral process will, hopefully, discourage any future use of suicide threats as manipulation. If your child is *not* using the threat of suicide as a manipulation and is, in fact, suicidal, taking that child to a crisis center is the appropriate action. Determine, ahead of time, which agency in your area is appropriate, and have the phone number ready.

Act More and Talk Less

Parents are notorious for talking too much and acting too little. Our own children now tell us they had given titles and numbers to the family lectures we gave. Lecture number one was, "Don't you see what you're doing to yourself?" Lecture number two was, "Don't you see what you're doing to this family?" Lecture number three was, "You're going to ruin your future." The kids even knew how long each lecture lasted. They would daydream during most of the talking and then snap back just as the lecture ended. Then they would say, "I see what you mean. That helps a lot." Then they would trot away. Nothing changed. The way to get kids' attention is by acting, not talking. One consequence is worth a thousand words. Consequences take us to Chapter Ten.

10. Follow Through with Consequences If the "No Use" Rule Is Broken

This chapter is the heart of a family drug prevention program. Chapter Two pointed out that early alcohol and other drug use is a matter of decision—kids use because they decide to use. Chapter Three pointed out kids decide to use alcohol and other drugs because it feels good.

Consequences interfere with those drug-induced good feelings and interrupt the cycle of drug use by creating discomfort for the user. Parents who don't provide consequences allow this cycle of drug use to continue uninterrupted. Parents who *do* follow through with consequences when the no use rule is broken intervene in the drug use cycle. The consequences clearly say, "Your decision to use alcohol and other drugs is unacceptable to me." Consequences give children an opportunity to learn from unacceptable decisions. When the consequences are applied to alcohol and other drug decisions, the lessons learned can be lifesaving. Following through with consequences when the no use rule is broken isn't a parent's option, it's a parent's responsibility.

Developing Creative Consequences

Many parents have told us they got stuck when it came to consequences. The consequences they gave their children were often limited to "grounding" or some other predictable action.

"But what else can I do? What other consequences can I give?" they asked.

Ray Nordine, executive director of Family Plus, Inc., in Minneapolis, says the secret of developing effective consequences is to get creative. He believes the basis of effective, creative consequences is in this simple sentence: *children want and need more from parents than parents want and need from their children.*

Ray suggests to parents that they write a list of the things their kids want from them and use that "Want List" to develop consequences.

We developed a Want List as part of each Parents' Program we presented around the country. We asked the audience, "What do kids want and need from parents?" Every time, without exception, the first answer parents called out to us was, "Love." Following that answer parents would say, "Understanding . . . support . . . spiritual and religious training . . . guidance . . . direction . . . "

As the parents called out their answers, we wrote them on a blackboard:

love
understanding
support
spiritual and religious training
guidance and direction

After five or six of these answers, we would stop and say, "Okay, these are pretty typical parent answers. They focus on the *needs.* Now let's list some *wants.* What do kids *want* from parents?"

This question usually stumped the parents. They would sit quietly, thinking. We would ask, "What would your kids say? What do kids really want?"

Then the answers would come faster than we could write them. "A stereo . . . money . . . a car . . . designer jeans . . . permission to stay out late . . . " We wrote these answers on the blackboard:

stereo
money
a car
designer jeans
permission to stay out late

Next, we separated the wants from the needs.

WANTS	NEEDS
stereo	love
money	support
car	understanding
jeans	spiritual and religious
stay out late	guidance and direction

Then we added to the needs list the things parents are *required* by law to provide for their children: food, shelter, clothing, medical attention, support, and guidance.

With that, the needs list stopped growing. But the want list continued to grow longer and longer as parents added all of the privileges and favors their kids want from them:

staying overnight at a friend's house
having parties at home
rides to ballgames and movies
cleaning their rooms

Finally, we had to stop writing when the want list filled the blackboard. "Now," we said, "if you want to develop effective consequences to influence drug decisions, look at the items on the want list as bargaining chips. That's where your power to influence drug decisions is based."

Consequences from a Want List Are Powerful Motivators

First, consequences developed from a want list will get a kid's attention. These consequences focus on privileges, possessions, and favors—things kids want. Kids listen when parents talk about withholding or removing these privileges. Kids listen because, as one parent told us, "Kids want their wants more than they want their needs." And, she said, "If you don't believe that, just ask your kids what they want more—love, understanding, and support . . . or a new stereo!"

Second, consequences developed from a want list are personal. Children may not relate to impersonal, clinical studies about the harmful effects of smoking marijuana, but they will relate to the loss of something they want.

Third, consequences developed from a want list can be the source of immediate action. Family therapists agree that consequences are most effective when they are immediate. What can be more immediate than the sudden withdrawal of a privilege?

Fourth, parents control these consequences because they control the items on the want list. It's true that kids control their own decisions about drug use—but parents can influence those decisions with consequences.

One night in New Mexico, we were talking about developing creative consequences by using the want list. We asked the parents in the audience if someone would give us a real-life example of something their chidren wanted—and how that want could be used to develop a creative consequence.

A mother raised her hand and said, "How about a door on his bedroom?" We asked her if she would tell the rest of us how she could use *that* to create a consequence around drug use.

She said, "Well, last night when I came home from work, I thought I smelled the odor of marijuana coming from my son's bedroom.

"But the door to his bedroom was closed, and I couldn't see what was happening. When I asked through the door what was going on, my son told me everything was fine. He said he was just talking with a couple of his friends. I didn't know what to do. I didn't want to open the door because that might embarrass him. Finally, I just went to bed.

"He wants that door. He wants it closed all of the time. I could use that want to develop a consequence by sitting him down and saying, 'Last night I thought I smelled the odor of marijuana coming from your bedroom. I don't ever want to smell that odor in my home again. If I *do* smell that odor in my home again, I'm going to take the door off your bedroom and put it down in the basement. Permanently!' "

That's creative. The door becomes the bargaining chip. Here's another example of developing a creative consequence. This one was created by a father in Minnesota who was concerned about the dangers of teenage drinking and driving.

A few days before this father's sixteen-year-old son was scheduled to take the road test for his driver's license, the father typed out the following letter:

Director, Drivers License Division
Minnesota Department of Motor Vehicles
Transportation Building
St. Paul, Minnesota 55101

Dear Director:

On November 22, 1982, I signed a form giving permission to the state of Minnesota to issue my sixteen-year-old son a Minnesota driver's license. Recently my son operated his automobile following the use of alcohol.

Based on my son's decision to use alcohol and drive, I withdraw that permission and request the immediate withdrawal of my son's driver's license.

Sincerely,

_____
Date

Then, with the letter in his hand, the father sat down with his son and said, "You've asked me to sign for you next week, giving permission for you to get a driver's license. I'm willing to do that, but first, I want to make one thing absolutely clear.

"It is my expectation that you will never drive while under the influence of alcohol or other drugs. If I ever find out, or suspect, you've driven a car while under the influence of drugs, I will withdraw my permission for you to have a driver's license. Now I want you to read this."

He gave his son the letter and waited until he had finished reading it. Then the father placed the letter into a stamped, addressed envelope, sealed the envelope, and put it in his desk drawer. He looked at his son and said, "If you abide by the no use rule, I'll never have to mail that letter. It will stay right here in my desk drawer."

The want list can also be used to develop consequences for behavior which isn't drug related. A friend of ours came to our home one night crying and upset. "I don't know what I'm going to do," she said. "My daughter's becoming a real problem. She won't do anything I ask her. She won't lift a hand to help around the house. Tonight I gave her three jobs to do while I went to the store. When I came back, she hadn't done any of them. What am I going to do?"

We said, "Let's brainstorm the situation and see if we can develop some creative consequences. What does she *want*? What does she like to do?"

"She loves to roller-skate," the mother said.

"Where does she get her money to skate?" we asked. "Do you give her an allowance?"

"No. I don't give her any money," the mother responded. "She baby-sits."

After discussing the possible consequences, the mother decided upon this: She would tell her daughter that the next time she failed to complete an assigned chore, she would be given a consequence. The mother's plan was to avoid arguing or nagging about uncompleted chores. She would do the work herself—and then as a consequence, charge the daughter for the work performed.

Just as the mother was leaving our house, she turned and asked, "But what if she refuses to pay me?"

"Go to the place she baby-sits and garnishee her wages!" we said.

The daughter paid once; after that she did the chores.

Guidelines for Consequences

Consequences need to be observable. Any time a parent gives a consequence, such as grounding or removing telephone privileges, the parents need to be present to assure the consequence is being honored. If you take away a telephone privilege, for example, you can set up the consequence by saying, "I can't keep you from using the phone when I'm not home, so your consequence will be no use of the telephone—anytime I am home—during the next two weeks."

Consequences need to be reasonable. Don't ground your child for a year—it's too hard on *you*.

Consequences can be changed. If, in anger, you *do* ground your child for a year, it's okay to explain to your child that you made a mistake and apologize. Then you can give new, more reasonable consequences.

Consequences don't need to be specified in advance. Some parents tell their kids, in advance, exactly what the consequence will be for each broken rule. That's like hanging a price tag on each rule. Kids can look at the price and then decide if they are willing to pay the price to break the rule. It's *not* necessary to tell your child what the consequences will be or when they will occur. It *is* necessary to tell your child that there will be a consequence if the no use rule is broken.

Following through with consequences is the heart of an effective family drug prevention program. Yet many parents don't follow through with consequences. Why don't they? That question takes us to Chapter Eleven.

11. Recognize What Stops Parents from Following Through with Consequences

(BILL)

If I had just one day to live over, it would be the day the principal of Coral Gables High School called me and said, "Mr. Perkins, your son Steve has just been arrested for possession and sale of marijuana here on our school campus. The police are taking him to the Dade County jail."

I listened in disbelief as the principal continued. "Mr. Perkins, the reason I'm calling is that Steve's arrest is not only a legal problem, it is also a school problem. Steve is a marginal student. If he misses many days of school as a result of being in jail, it's likely he'll fail his junior year here at Coral Gables High." I listened numbly until I heard the principal's voice saying good-bye. Then I dropped the phone to the table. I could feel my desperation rising.

I loved my son; I couldn't let that happen; I couldn't let him fail. I immediately called an attorney and that afternoon we bailed Steve out of jail. Within a few days the attorney managed to get all of the charges against Steve dropped.

That was many years ago. Since then I've learned more about alcohol, other drugs, and kids. If I had to make that decision today, I would consider leaving my son in the Dade County jail. I say that because today I know children are always learning from parents—and my son learned two things from me the day I bailed him out of jail.

First, he learned I was a liar. I had told him if he didn't stop "messing around" with alcohol and other drugs, something bad would happen to him. But the first time something did happen, I stepped in and took away his opportunity to learn from the consequences of drug abuse. Steve learned my words were empty. Nothing bad was going to happen as a result of his drug use.

My son learned a second lesson that day. He learned if he *did* use drugs and he did get into trouble, someone else would take responsibility for his decisions. Someone else would bail him out. Someone else would clean up the mess. Sadly, he learned those lessons well. Steve continued to use drugs and find people who would insulate him from the problems caused by his drug use. He did that until, as he told me recently, he was almost dead.

Why didn't I leave my son in the Dade County jail? What stopped me from doing what I knew was best for my son? I've asked myself those questions many times over the years. I've found some answers, and some of those answers are difficult to admit, even to myself. I wish I could simply say, "I did it because I loved him." Certainly that's one of the reasons. But there are other reasons that don't have anything to do with love. They have to do with fear, pride, selfishness, and ego.

There are sometimes good reasons for not *automatically* leaving children in jail or not refusing to let them come home. Those reasons may include legal responsibilities to provide support at these times. But the *main consideration* should be the child's welfare, and parents should seek advice from legal and health care professionals in deciding exactly how their children should experience consequences. The ultimate goal should be to get their children to accept help or consequences, not just to punish them.

I've talked with other parents about why I didn't allow Steve to experience the consequences of his drug use. Many of the parents I talked to said they, too, rescued their children for reasons similar to mine. Together, we wrote down the reasons we didn't follow through with consequences. Here are some of those reasons:

We Were Afraid of Being Judged by Family and Friends

When the principal of Coral Gables High told me that Steve had been arrested, I felt terrible pain. Much of my pain came from my own feelings of shame. At that time we lived in an upper-middle-class neighborhood, and I thought our neighbors were happy, loving, and free from problems. I wanted them to think our family was happy too, but I knew that if I left Steve in jail they would find out about it. I knew they would talk among themselves, saying I was a bad parent. I wanted to avoid that; I was ashamed of what was happening in our family. I wanted to stop my feelings of shame, so I got my son out of jail and told myself I did it for his sake.

We Were Concerned about Our Professional Reputations

I worked for a conservative Fortune 500 company with a strong code of conduct for employees and the families of employees. I knew that my opportunities at work would be affected if it was discovered that my son had been arrested for using and selling drugs. In order to protect myself, I took away an opportunity for my son to learn a vital lesson about alcohol and other drugs.

We Were Too Busy

We were too busy to take time out of our lives for court appearances, school meetings, and all of the other inconveniences which would have resulted from Steve's jailing, trial, and failure at school. It was easier on us, less demanding on our time, just to get him out of jail and go on with our lives.

We Wanted to Avoid Our Children's Reactions

Whenever Nancy or I took any parenting action which our kids didn't like, the kids reacted. They reacted with

Threats
Anger
Guilt

We called it "Playing Tag," and it often became a vicious, punishing game.

Threats

Children's threats include quitting school, running away, hurting themselves, suicide, and physical abuse to parents. Many parents are stopped by their children's threats and don't follow through with consequences. Threats should be taken seriously, but parents should not give in to them.

Anger

Some parents told us they were afraid of their children's anger, and they would do almost anything to avoid a confrontation. But they said they paid a high price for their failure to take action: they had to live with the problems they wouldn't confront.

Behavior which was originally unacceptable got worse. A few broken rules became many broken rules. Coming in late for curfew became staying out all night. Verbal abuse became physical abuse. The intention was to avoid an angry situation, but it didn't work because an out-of-control kid *is* an angry kid.

Guilt

Guilt is another way my kids stopped me, and I had a reservoir of guilt for them to use. I had been an active alcoholic during most of the years my children were growing up. My alcoholism put my children through experiences that were living nightmares.

Let me share just one example with you. When my son Danny was four years old, he was a sweet, blond-haired, blue-eyed kid. One night, when I was drunk, Danny said something or did something to make me angry. I don't even remember what it was. I swung my hand to hit him, but he ran. That made me even more angry, so I chased him to his room where he hid under his bed. I grabbed him by the ankle and pulled him from beneath the bed. The force of my pulling spun him around and his head hit one of the bed legs. As I watched, a deep gash opened on his forehead.

Today Danny carries a scar that I put there when I was in an alcoholic rage, something I still feel guilty about. That guilt almost kept me from taking action when Danny was eighteen years old and needed help but didn't want it. Over a period of months Danny had been changing from a laughing, cooperative, sensitive young man to a sullen, withdrawn, and angry person. He sat watching television and resisted looking for a job. He wouldn't even talk about going to college. His life was stalled out.

As things got worse, I talked with him, lectured him, and fought with him. He didn't seem to hear—or care. Finally, when I knew that nothing I was saying was having any effect, I knew I had to take action. I told Danny I expected him to get a job and find a place to live on his own within the next three months.

His eyes filled with tears, he said, "Dad, this is just one more thing you're doing to make my life miserable. You made life miserable for me when you were drinking—and you're making life miserable for me now that you're sober. Why don't you get off my back?"

When I saw the tears in his eyes, I remembered the child I had hurt so many times before. Guilt swept over me, telling me to stop.

We Were Afraid of the Unknown

Not long after that, Danny moved into an apartment near a bridge where many of the jumper suicides take place in St. Paul. I couldn't sleep, thinking about that bridge. I saw Danny, alone, looking down into the deep night waters. Then I received a telephone call that heightened all of my fears.

The call came from a counselor who had recently completed a psychological evaluation on Danny. He told me the evaluation indicated Danny was suffering from depression. Instantly, in my mind, I saw that bridge. I heard myself saying, "You've got to go get him. . . . You've got to bring him home where he'll be safe."

My fear of what might happen—my fear of the unknown—was telling me that I had to do something, I had to step in. But I didn't.

Danny was getting counseling and guidance. He was learning to take care of himself. He was growing. I realize that any suicidal comments or warnings should not be ignored. Nor should parents assume that because a person is getting counseling, the counselor is able to handle a potential suicide. All potential suicides should be referred to a suicide prevention specialist. Fortunately, Danny did not attempt suicide.

We Felt Sorry for Our Kids

I feel *sad* about what happened to my children. I feel sad for all children who get involved with alcohol and other drugs. But I no longer feel *sorry* for them. The two feelings are very different. Feeling sorry for kids often excuses them from responsible behavior and consequences. Feeling sorry for kids has a language all of its own. Listen to the way it discounts kids:

"You can't handle it. I'll take care of it for you."
"You can't take the pain. I'll get you out of it."
"You're not smart enough. I'll figure it out for you."
"You can't do it. I'll have to do it for you."

Let's not discount our kids by excusing them from responsible behavior.

They can handle it!
They are smart enough!
They are tough enough!
They can do it!

Parents also stop consequences because they don't clearly understand their parenting responsibilities.

Defining the job of parenting takes us to Chapter Twelve.

12. Understand the Job of Parenting

Many parents told us their job as a parent often left them feeling angry, powerless, and out of control.

"I don't know what to do!" they said in exasperation. "Parenting is the hardest job I've ever had."

One night in Ashland, Wisconsin, a frustrated parent said, "What we need are some guidelines to parenting . . . we need a job description!"

During the next few weeks we thought about a job description for parents and asked other parents what they thought should be included in a parent's job description. Based on those suggestions and adapted from "The Four Laws of Parenting Responsibility" by Ray Nordine, here it is:

A Parent's Job Description

Parents have the responsibility to build and maintain a functional family structure in which both children and parents can grow, learn, thrive, and move toward their full God-given potential.

Parents have the responsibility to teach and guide their children to develop the skills, strength, and knowledge they will need to take care of themselves in the real adult world.

Parents have the responsibility to require their children to decide and act in a responsible manner.

Anytime a parent accepts responsibility for those things which are the child's responsibility, that child doesn't have to accept responsibility for himself or herself. An opportunity to learn and develop the skills, strengths, and knowledge they will need to take care of themselves in the real, adult world is lost.

Build and maintain a functional family structure. Develop family rules, set limits, and be consistent. That sounds easy enough, doesn't it?

But now let's give our kids a job description. Then we'll see why a parent's job isn't as easy as it sounds. A kid's job description is just two words long:

Test Everything

Testing everything begins when our children are a few months old. Anything you hand an infant—or anything an infant can get their hands on—goes right into their mouth. They're checking out a new and mysterious world.

When kids get older, their world gets bigger. Parents begin saying things like, "Don't leave the yard." Or, "Don't go into the street." At some point, alcohol and other drugs enter a kid's world; many kids will test that, too. That's why 90 percent of the kids in America have used alcohol or other drugs before they graduate from high school. They're not bad, or drug oriented; they're curious and testing.

A parent's job is to build and maintain, develop the guidelines, set the rules, and enforce the limits. A kid's job is to test it all. That's why parents and kids are on an unavoidable collision course. It's a natural, normal, and blameless process.

Parents who have most successfully navigated through the parent and child collision course are those who have regularly checked their parenting and who have been willing to make changes when changes were needed. That takes us to Chapter Thirteen.

13. Be Willing to Make Parenting Changes

(NANCY)

Years ago I went into counseling to see what I could do to change my kids. I remember telling my counselor, "If only my kids would change, everything would be alright." I was shocked when the counselor didn't agree with me. She said, "Nancy, you need to take the focus off the kids and put it on yourself. If you want your family to be healthy, changes need to begin with you."

I discovered in counseling I had never taken the time to figure out who I was or what I wanted. I just let things happen. There was no structure in my life or in my parenting. I moved between passive and aggressive parenting.

Passive Parenting

Because there was no structure in my parenting, I set few rules and I was unclear about my expectations. I found it difficult to communicate directly. I thought my children should know what I wanted from them without my telling them. Because I was unwilling to be direct with my children, I often used guilt and helplessness to manipulate them to get what I wanted. I had a terrible time making the smallest decisions. I was indecisive about everything. When my children would ask if they could go somewhere or do something, I would first say "no" and then say "yes."

My children reacted to my passive parenting by ignoring me, talking back to me, and treating me with contempt and disrespect. My feelings were often hurt, but I wouldn't talk about it. I would keep my feelings inside until I couldn't hold them back any longer, and then I would explode. The explosion would hurl me from the extreme of being a passive parent to the extreme of being an aggressive parent.

Aggressive Parenting

When I was parenting aggressively, I became a rigid and demanding rule maker. I was going to get everything in our family shaped up—right now—today. My communications went from indirect to abusive. I used anger, threats, and intimidation to get what I wanted. I went from indecisive to inflexible. When I said something, that was it! There were no discussions. All my feelings of hurt, disappointment, and fear were converted to anger and rage. My children reacted to my aggressive parenting by avoiding me, placating me, and trying to be extra nice in order to subdue my anger. When I saw how my aggressive parenting was affecting my children, I would feel remorse. Filled with shame, I would lapse back into my passive parenting, promising myself I would never act like that again.

But I couldn't keep those promises, and the cycle continued. I really wanted to change the way I was parenting, but I didn't know how. Then, in a book I was reading, I discovered the characteristics of assertiveness. I made a decision to become an assertive parent.

Assertive Parenting

I began working on my assertive parenting by taking time out for myself. I had never done that before. In the past, I would jump out of bed in the morning and rush into my day, gaining speed as the day went on. The faster I moved, the easier it was for me to avoid looking at myself.

Now I began to take time for myself each morning. I set the alarm so I could get up earlier than the rest of the family. I took time to reflect on what my behavior had been like the day before and how I wanted to behave during the day ahead.

I wanted to learn how to be a loving parent, a patient parent, and so I would start each day by telling myself, "Today I am going to practice being patient." I would write notes reminding myself to be patient. Then I would tape the notes to the refrigerator, mirrors, and doors.

Often, during my aggressive parenting, I would come home from work expecting the kids to have washed the dishes, made the beds, and vacuumed the rugs. When this work wasn't done, I would get angry and yell. But as I began practicing patience, I would stop before going into the house and say to myself, "Now you know the dishes aren't going to be done, and the beds aren't going to be made, and the rugs won't be vacuumed. You have a choice. You can go in there and yell, or you can practice patience."

Once I became aware of what I was doing—and that I had choices about how I behaved—I began to make some progress. When I got through a day successfully practicing patience, I would give myself credit. It wasn't long before I was having more patient days than impatient days.

When I began to feel good about the progress I was making with being patient, I decided to go to work on another area of my parenting. I decided to work on listening. Somewhere I had gotten the idea children were to be seen and not heard, and their ideas and thoughts were not important. Because I believed this, I discounted my children and what they were saying. I didn't listen to them.

I started to change this by making myself available to my children. If I was busy when they came to me, I would stop what I was doing, sit down, make eye contact, and *really listen* to what they were saying. This was a difficult task at first. It took time and patience. I'm grateful now that I took the time and had the patience to listen. I learned things about my children I never knew before. I learned that they are bright, creative, and funny. I discovered how much I enjoyed their company. I also found out they knew all of the family secrets, all of the things I thought I had successfully kept from them through the years.

Listening brought me another awareness. I became aware that when I spoke to my children, I was often abrupt, demanding, and condescending. I spoke to strangers with more respect than I spoke to my own children. The way I changed may seem silly, but it worked for me. I played a game of pretend. While I was talking to my children, I would ask myself, "If this were a friend or co-worker how would I be talking to them? What tone of voice would I use? How would I act?" Then I would pretend that my kids *were* these people. Rather than demand, I began to ask. Rather than take them for granted, I began to say "please" and "thank you." I changed the tone in my voice. I worked to speak slower, softer, and with more warmth. As I warmed up, my kids warmed up.

The next thing I needed to work on was keeping my promises. My children might ask me on Monday if I would take them to the movies Saturday. Without thinking, I would say, "Sure." Then Saturday would roll around, and the kids would ask, "Are we going to the movies today?" I would answer in a surprised voice, "Movie? Today? I can't go to a movie today, I'm too busy." Because I didn't keep my promises, the kids learned not to trust me.

To change this, I made a decision to THINK before answering their questions. Thinking before speaking helped me keep my promises. Keeping my promises improved my credibility. Improving my credibility allowed me to develop other areas of my assertive parenting. I was better able to develop the structure which had been lacking in my personal and family life. I began to communicate directly and honestly. I set rules and became clear about my expectations. I began to follow through with consequences for unacceptable behavior. And I began expressing my feelings and needs openly.

One of the first needs I became aware of was my need to be a nurturing, affectionate parent. While my children were growing up, my passive and aggressive parenting had caused me to miss out on many opportunities to nurture. I often wished I could do something to regain those lost opportunities.

Then one day I heard something that allowed me to stop wishing and start doing. In a psychology course I was taking, the instructor said, "If you missed being nurtured in your past, it's okay to ask someone to nurture you now. You can ask someone to hug you, hold you, or stroke you. You can ask for whatever you missed."

I was fascinated by the idea. I thought about it for days, then I decided to take a risk. I decided to ask my children to allow me to give them, now, the nurturing I missed giving them earlier. That would be risky for me. The kids might reject me. They were tired and frustrated with all the new behavior changes I was making. Try to envision what happened when I went to my daughter Kelly, who was fifteen at the time, and asked, "Would you let me hold you and rock you?"

She froze in her tracks and stared at me in disbelief. I could see from the expression on her face that she thought I had finally gone completely crazy. But she didn't say a word; she just looked long and hard at me. Then, slowly, the disbelief left her face. She continued to look into my eyes, even harder. To my surprise, she said, "Okay."

I felt nervous as I held out my hand to her. Kelly, too, appeared guarded as she moved closer. Slowly, cautiously, she sat down on my lap. We had been sitting for only a moment when I began to panic. I wanted to push her away. This was *too* close.

I began talking to myself. "Relax . . . it'll be alright . . . you'll get through these uncomfortable feelings . . . just don't push her away."

My panic lasted no more than 60 seconds, but it seemed like 60 minutes. Finally, I relaxed. The two of us sat there for a long time, not saying a word. Just being close, holding each other, healing. It was wonderful.

Taking a risk with Kelly allowed me to begin reaching out to the boys. I started slowly. At first, I would touch their hand or arm, just making light contact. Then I got the courage to ask for a hug. Like Kelly, they said, "Okay." Nurturing and hugging felt warm and healing to me. I could tell the kids liked it, too.

As the process of my recovery as a parent continued, I was able to look more honestly at myself and make other needed changes. Previously, my parenting had focused on the negative. I didn't see my children's positive behavior. As a result, I gave them very little praise or verbal support.

My son Tim had always been a high achiever. He had received good grades all through school. He had taught himself how to play several musical instruments and had formed his own band in high school. As a result of this hard work and musical ability, he won a scholarship to college. He worked his way through four years of undergraduate school and then through three years of law school. He was always responsible and self-sufficient. He never asked us for anything. And yet Tim was the child in our family who received the least amount of praise and verbal support.

When I became aware of this, I made a decision to express to Tim my love, support, and appreciation for who he was and what he was doing. I began to look for ways I could praise and support all the children. If a task was completed, I complimented them for it. When their rooms were clean, I praised them. I began commenting on their good qualities—their thoughtfulness, helpfulness, their caring, and concern. I praised their insights, intelligence, and abilities. I made a point of finding at least one good thing to say about each child, each day. Where I used to put them down, I now worked to build them up.

And the kids responded. I could see it. Almost daily, I could see them gaining confidence, a sense of self-worth, and feelings of security. The investment of time and energy to become an assertive parent was now paying dividends.

During the time I was working on making changes in myself, I wrote daily reminder notes about what I needed to become a more assertive parent. Finally, to get some room on my refrigerator door, I compiled all of the notes into the following:

Assertive Parenting Checklist
- Do I practice patience?
- Do I *really listen* to my kids?

- Am I considerate of my children's feelings?
- Do I speak to my children with respect?
- Do I keep promises?
- Am I honest with my children?
- Do I stay open and flexible?
- Do I communicate family values?
- Do I set appropriate limits?
- Have I clearly stated family rules?
- Do I enforce the family rules with consequences?
- Can I say "no" (or "yes") when I need to?
- Am I consistent?
- Do I give my kids choices?
- Do I assist my children in decision making and problem solving?
- Do I support? encourage? nurture? praise?
- Do I laugh and play and have fun with my children?

What I learned during the time I was working to change myself is that love is not just a word. *Love is the energy it takes to be present and working on a relationship.*

Afterword

We've covered a lot of information in this book—prevention through nutrition, educating yourself, preparing for alcohol and other drug use, intervening on that use, creating consequences, and making changes in the way we parent. Following these steps is going to take a lot of work, and you're going to make a lot of mistakes. You're not going to do it perfectly. But that's okay!

All the parents we talked to around America told us they made lots of mistakes. But they didn't quit. They stuck to it. They called a friend or went to a parents' meeting. They reached out to get the support and courage to continue.

When we told these parents that we were writing a book, they told us to tell you, "Forgive yourself." "Hang in there." "Parents are going to make the difference in this drug-filled world."

That is our prayer, too: that all of us, together, can show our children the way to healthy, vital, drug-free lives. It's a long and continuing journey, but like all journeys, it begins with the first step.

We hope to meet you somewhere along the way.

Until then, God bless you all.

Bibliography

Atkins, Robert C., M.D. *Dr. Atkins' Nutrition Breakthrough.* New York: William Morrow and Company, Inc., 1981.

Cheraskin, E., W. M. Ringsdorf, and J. W. Clark. *Diet and Disease.* New Canaan, Conn.: Keats Publishing, 1968.

Feingold, Ben F., M.D. *Why Your Child Is Hyperactive.* New York: Random House, 1974.

Fredericks, Carlton. *Nutrition Handbook.* Huntington Beach, Calif.: International Institute of Natural Health Sciences, Inc., 1976.

Goodwin, D. W. *Is Alcoholism Hereditary?* New York: Oxford University Press, 1976.

Ketcham, Katherine, and L. Ann Mueller, M.D. *Eating Right to Live Sober.* Seattle, Wa.: Madrona Publishers, 1983.

Kunin, Richard A. *Mega Nutrition for Women.* New York: McGraw-Hill, 1983.

Land, Donald R., Ph.D., and Sandra Cohen-Homes, M.Ed. *Focus on Family and Chemical Dependency* 7, 2 (March/April 1984): 10.

Mandell, Marshall, M.D., and Lynne W. Scanlon. *Dr. Mandell's Five Day Allergy Relief System.* New York: Thomas Y. Crowell, 1979.

Mason, Jeanette. *Alcoholism, The National Magazine,* Spring 1984, 47.

Null, Gary, with Steven Null. *The New Vegetarian.* New York: Dell Publishing Co., Inc., 1978.

Pfeiffer, Carl C., Ph.D., M.D., *Mental and Elemental Nutrients.* New Canaan, Conn.: Keats Publishing, Inc., 1975.

Philpott, William H., and Dwight K. Kalin. *Brain Allergies: The Psychonutrient Connection.* New Canaan, Conn.: Keats Publishing, Inc., 1980.

Poulos, C. Jean, Ph.D., D.Sc., Donald Stoddard, Ph.D., and Kathryn Carron. *The Relationship of Stress to Hypoglycemia and Alcoholism.* Huntington Beach, Calif.: International Institute of Natural Health Sciences, Inc., 1979.

Randolph, Theron G., M.D. and Ralph W. Moss, Ph.D. *An Alternative Approach to Allergies.* New York: Lippincott & Crowell, 1980.

Rapp, Doris, M.D. *Allergies and the Hyperactive Child.* New York: Sovereign, 1979.

Rapp, Doris, M.D. *Allergies and Your Family.* New York: Sterling Publishing Co., 1980.

Reed, Barbara. *Food, Teens and Behavior.* Manitowoc, Wisc.: Natural Press, 1980.

Smith, Lendon, M.D. *Feed Your Kids Right.* New York: Dell Publishing Co., Inc., 1979.

Williams, Roger J. *Nutrition Against Disease: Environmental Prevention.* New York: Pittman, 1971.